MW01034722

God Helped Us
Smuggle Hash

God Helped Us Smuggle Hash

An unusual true story of hippies in the 1960s
and the unorthodox love story
that complicated it

Pepper Sweet

Copyright © 2015 by Pepper Sweet
All rights reserved.

This is a work of creative nonfiction. The events are portrayed to the best of human memory, which is deeply flawed. It's almost impossible to recall a conversation word for word. While all the stories in this book are true, some names and identifying details have been changed to protect the privacy of the people involved. Additionally, any photo used in this book does not indicate that the person or people in the photo had any involvement in this story.

ISBN: 1515310663
ISBN 13: 9781515310662

ACKNOWLEDGMENTS

A friend of mine named Ty, who knows a lot about writing, read my first draft and told me I needed to find someone who can help me with my grammar, my tenses, and my sentence structure. It was disastrous, he said. Thanks for taking the time to read it and for the indispensable advice.

Just days later, I was on the phone with a high school friend, David Sydnor, who I hadn't spoken to in maybe forty years. I am not quite sure how we connected. After talking for quite a while, I mentioned I was writing a book. He asked if I would like some help. "Sure, what kind of help can you offer?"

"I was an English major; I can help you with grammar, tenses and sentence structure."

I love "coincidences" like that. Thank you, David, for hanging in there, page by page, two times through.

Also a big thanks to Penny King, who was honest and skilled enough to point out inconsistencies and poorly stated concepts and give good solutions. Bernard Beranger, all the way from Marseille, France, thanks for encouraging me to go through the book one more time and make some key parts clearer. Thanks to my three children who help me to not be so heavenly minded that I am no earthly good.

To the Divine, who brought my comatose heart to life and inspired the title of this book when I couldn't get started without knowing where I was going.

To all my friends, who are gracious and confused enough to love me and count me valuable, I hope to pass it forward.

Most of all, a tribute to my wife, who inspires, challenges, and questions me until it hurts, with the result being new insights and better communication. Without you I would be all facts and little emotion. You helped raise my emotional intelligence from the lowest levels, and thanks to you I find joy in embracing the sensitive side of life. This book does not exist without you. You are the best.

Profits from the sale and distribution of this book will be used exclusively in Non Profit Organizations dedicated to improving the quality of life to those with little opportunity.

For more information or to connect with the author, go to godhelpedussmugglehash.com

TABLE OF CONTENTS

CHAPTER 1

QUIEN ES ESE TIPO?

I wonder what sort of tale we have fallen into?

—J.R.R. Tolkien

There is something about being young that allows you to do crazy things without accurately assessing the risks or considering the consequences. We were definitely in that state of mind, making choices that involved little or no analytical reasoning, yet with potentially catastrophic results. Looking back, it is frightening. At the time, we just went with the flow.

For those of you who haven't seen *Butch Cassidy and the Sundance Kid*, it was a movie that came out in 1969 starring Robert Redford and Paul Newman. They robbed banks and trains in the old west. Their specialty was evading any posse that pursued them. They were masters at covering their trail. Almost always on horseback, they would ride down rivers, cross mountains, or disappear into Mexico and even as far as Bolivia, shaking off their less talented or less motivated pursuers. Then one day, it wasn't so easy. They were tracked by a posse with an extraordinary leader they couldn't shake. Time and again their wiliest tricks failed to deter the little band that stubbornly dogged their trail. At one point, as they looked over a rock in the mountains only to see that posse still on their trail, the question surfaced between them, "Who is that guy?"

I saw this movie in 1969, while living in Mexico City. The Spanish subtitle was "Quien es ese tipo?" Over the course of that chase, as their dismay and apprehensions grew, they repeated it to each other many times. They had always been able to get away, but now "that guy," whoever he was, seemed almost superhuman. Nothing fooled him. Then they would look at each other again and again with an increasing incredulity, "Quien es ese tipo?" Who is that guy? Ultimately "that guy" tracked them down to their demise.

And that is the nature of my story, or our story, as many on our journey recognized the same thing. Someone was tracking us. But in our case it was a friendly tracker. Someone was on our side. Experience after experience gave us the same message.

We had no idea who or what, but the sense that grew among us was that It or He or She was divine. It had to be. Too many times something would happen that was so far outside the norm that it hinted of the Divine. It wasn't exactly like the Red Sea opening, but there was enough that went down that it had a similar effect.

We knew we were in some kind of story. It was like when Sam left the Hollow and said to Frodo in *The Lord of the Rings*, as they approached Mordor, "I wonder what sort of tale we have fallen into?" They knew something larger than themselves was going on and that somehow they were a part of it; somehow they had "fallen into it." We knew the same thing, though ours was a much less epic tale. We were being helped, we were being rescued, and the end of our tale seemed to us a bright and happy one. Our mission was for good; we were helping to "turn on" the world, and we sensed we had Divine help, which made it all the more glorious. And everyone with us was enjoying the journey, the adventure. And what an adventure it was. But I am getting ahead of myself, so let me go back a few years.

CHAPTER 2

TWO LIFE-CHANGING DECISIONS

Then you better start swimmin' or you'll sink like a stone For the times they are a changin'

—Bob Dylan

My name is Justin Case. Apparently my parents never realized that those two names together could sound like "just in case" and would become the source of much ridicule throughout my youth. But it did. Kids can be brutal. I fought or fled, depending on the size of the kid mocking me.

I've lain awake in bed wondering where my story should begin. It could be in New Canaan, Connecticut, my home town, a wealthy community where most of our fathers commuted to New York City every morning by car or on the train. It could begin at Andover, a prestigious, elitist boarding school ("prep" school) in Massachusetts where George Bush was a classmate of mine and the head cheerleader. It could begin in Mexico, where I first discovered the third world and the tropics and wonderful, simple people and beaches and marijuana. It could begin in San Francisco, where I had a sandal shop on Haight Street. It could begin in Morocco, a culture and world so different it was as if we had stepped into Tolkien's trilogy and Hobbit land, where we lived for almost three years during the height of the Vietnam War era. But I am going to begin it at Lake Forest College, a small university in a wealthy town much like New Canaan, except located north of Chicago instead of New York City.

Lake Forest

The year was 1967, and the significance of my choice after almost three years at college was simple. It was the first time in my life that I made a conscious decision to be who I was. Not that anyone at age twenty knows who they are, but sometimes you find a root that seems real to you and something inside pushes you to be honest to that core value; though none of those words or ideas are really that clear at the time, you go with it and it feels right.

I had excelled in some sports in high school. You might say I was some sort of a jock. In college, being an athlete on one or more varsity teams awarded me inclusion into a certain clique. I played on the varsity team in both ice hockey and tennis and ended up in the most elite fraternity house of jocks and prep school graduates on campus; at least we thought so. It became my culture, my circle of friends, and my social network. It was there that I partied and hung out and fit in and established who I was.

But something changed, and I have wondered exactly how it happened. This much I remember always: In my junior year (the year I would eventually drop out and head to a hippie commune before moving on to Mexico), I was no longer getting drunk on the weekends, and even during the week. I had traded the beer for marijuana. And for some reason, that made me more introspective. In high school, my good friend Pete Grayson and I would get drunk and go to parties and be obnoxious and belligerent and often get in fights. At least Pete did. He was small, but a tempest in a teapot, and could beat up almost anyone of any size. When Pete and I turned to getting stoned, the fights stopped and "peace and love" was more the mantra. I became more aware, not only of the world outside, but also inside of myself. This was new for me. Sports, girls, and drinking had dominated my life; I gave no thought to anything else. Why should I? That was my world and I was happy in it.

Furthermore, the Vietnam War was beginning to reach its hand into every young male's life, confronting us with a question that under normal circumstances most young men don't have to answer. "Shall I go to war, pick up a gun and shoot and be shot at for a reason that no one could clearly identify?" It forced many of us to think. An antiwar movement was developing that would soon grow exponentially. The young people would lead it, and many of our parents' generation would support it, while others would not. The nation became divided. The civil rights movement was emerging at the same time, further dividing the country. And somehow getting drunk and partying and taking the elite stance (just do what's best for yourself) began to fade away.

Over time, I made two important decisions, which turned out to be life changing. The first was to quit my fraternity. It seemed like the right thing to do. They really were a good bunch of guys, apparently comfortable in the social culture in which they found themselves. They were my friends and we had a good time together. I would enjoy seeing and reminiscing with them today. But something was stirring within me and I could no longer ignore it.

I think it was the sense of elitism. When we would go to bars or sit around the fraternity house and drink, there was always someone to put down. I did my share of it. Racial, gender, cultural, and socio-economic slurs were not common, but they weren't rare, either, especially as blood alcohol levels grew. It sort of crept up on me. I just didn't want to be part of the mentality of superiority anymore. I could feel that in my roots. It was no longer who I was. I felt like I was crossing an internal line when I participated in disrespecting others. My sympathies were increasingly drawn toward those who were my fellowman but discriminated against for the color of their skin or their country of origin. My heart responded to the civil rights movement and Martin Luther King Jr. I was opposed to the war in Vietnam. I was realizing that I was no better than anyone else. I was not an elitist at heart. Although I probably couldn't have expressed any of this in words at the time, I felt it. And even though it would completely change my social network, and ultimately undermine my existence at college, I would go with it.

It was my first decision in life to be real, to begin to discover who I was. It made me feel alive and genuine for the first time. It was almost like a religious conversion, although I had no religion or belief in God. I had lost what little faith I might have had at Andover. But something inside had changed. That much I knew. I just couldn't verbalize it. It was too new to me.

Andover

And now I need to take you back to Andover for a moment. Andover was one of the most elite prep schools in the country. It is where the "cream of the crop" go as they prepare for Harvard, Yale, Princeton, or MIT. Many of the top athletes who graduate from high school, but can't make it into the elite colleges, go to Andover to prepare themselves for that step. Some of the smartest kids in the nation are there, and a few of the richest. There are a lot of names I could drop that went to Andover. It never really impressed me.

In fact, my family never struck me as anything special, but looking back, it was an impressive group of relatives: members of Congress, judges, community leaders, pioneers in many fields. Perhaps our most famous family member was Charles Carroll of Carrollton, who was the only Roman Catholic to sign the Declaration of Independence. He was a strong advocate of separation from Great Britain, and a leader in the Revolution. I think some of his spirit passed on to me, though sometimes used for less noble purposes.

My dad was one of those athletes who couldn't get into Yale out of high school, so he went to Andover and then on to Yale. The list of my relatives that went to Yale was long enough to get me in on my heritage alone. Andover would also help punch my ticket to Yale. But I didn't like Andover. Perhaps it was going to an all-boys school, or maybe it was my inability to excel with so much competition, intellectually and athletically. It could have been that my assigned roommate made life difficult for me, or that I just wasn't ready to leave home yet. I think many may have felt uneasy and vulnerable, but no one would ever dare to talk about it. That would have been way too risky.

On top of that, we were required to go to chapel every morning and we all had to take a Bible class sophomore year. The intellectual atheists dominated. They seemed much better prepared with their atheistic arguments than the teacher himself. He may have been an atheist, too, for all I know, as he put up little defense. After a full semester of it, I think the whole class emerged atheists. Although I had never given much thought to God or religion, it sort of eliminated any possibility of His existence and it didn't bother me. I didn't care. I don't know if it added additional bleakness to my state of mind, but it was a miserable sophomore year.

Junior year was somewhat better. I made some great friends in the dorm. I was a good card player, especially bridge. My bridge partner, John Hunter...well, we dominated. That was an accomplishment at Andover. Anything you could dominate at Andover was saying something. We had many of the best in every category including the most accomplished cynics. The competition at every level was intense. And we were brainwashed to believe that we were the elite of the elite.

Somehow, I didn't really buy into it. I preferred to just be a regular guy. I wanted to go home to my high school, which was already a fairly elite high school in the wealthiest town in America at that time. My neighbors were like a list of the Forbes Fortune 500 though I don't think the list was well known at the time. My dad was President and CEO of an international trading company on Madison Avenue in New York City, though I never felt like we were the upper crust of New Canaan, especially since we were not "old money." It seemed like most of the town commuted on the train to New York City every day. Many of them were Yale, Harvard, and Princeton graduates. But it was nothing compared to the elitism of Andover. High school was much more a mixture of people, and I had a girlfriend there. Oh, what hormones and a girl can do. I wanted to go home.

My parents were confused, distraught, and incensed at the idea, especially my dad. There must be something wrong with me. Why would anyone want to leave Andover? I must be mentally sick in some way. So they took me to a psychiatrist. Dr. Maziltoff was a female psychiatrist, somewhat unusual for that time. She was a friend of my mom. I think she helped my mom manage some tough times with my dad. He wasn't the easiest father and as a husband...well, I saw my mom cry a few times. He was a strong personality, and she was, too.

When we arrived at her office, Dr. Maziltoff spoke to me alone first in her office. She tried to determine why I would want to leave Andover and go home for my senior year.

"What is it that you don't like about Andover?" she queried. *"What makes you feel uncomfortable there?"*

I don't remember all that I said, but I was honest with her and it wasn't a hard question for me.

"First of all it's an all-boys school. You have to go to chapel every morning. You walk long distances to classes as each class is in a different building on a huge campus, and its cold most of the year, bitter cold sometimes. You eat every meal in a cafeteria with all the other guys. You have to wear a coat and tie to class, and virtually everywhere. You have to walk a mile into town with your dirty clothes to do your laundry. You never see your family. There are no parties on the weekends, no dating. My best friends are here in New Canaan, not there."

When I finally paused she commented. *"In other words, there is nothing there that reminds you of home."*

It wasn't quite the way I would have put it, but I could at least agree with her.

She sent me out of her office so she could speak with my parents. Finally, we all met together for what I figured was certain to be a verdict in favor of my parents. I was ready to fight. I had already threatened that if they forced me back I would get myself kicked out. And that would be easy. I had already done enough damage at Andover on drunken escapades to get kicked out, but never got caught. I knew what to do, and it would be easy to get caught.

To my astonishment, Dr. Maziltoff spoke words I had never heard come out of an adult's mouth. I am quite certain I had never heard a supportive comment from anyone over forty years old before. My parents were both very driven, and nothing was ever good enough. Or at least that's the way it felt. I was always a little short of what I was supposed to be. Although a good athlete and a good student, I wasn't good enough. It will lead a young man to drink, a skill I had indeed mastered. Anyway, her summary judgment was ready. Dr. Maziltoff's words were stunning. She looked at my parents and in a professional voice she spoke to all of us:

"It is not abnormal for a boy to want to be at home and around his friends and family."

And that was it, end of conversation. I was coming home. Thank you Dr. Maziltoff!

New Canaan High

New Canaan High, my senior year, was my idea of a blast. I had a girl-friend, knew how to party and was drunk almost every weekend, which was the norm for a lot of us. If it hadn't been for sports, I would have been drinking after school as well, which I did whenever I could. The drinking age in Connecticut was twenty one, but eighteen in New York; New Canaan bordered the New York State line on one side. So it was common for many of us to head to New York and buy beer at a liquor store just across the line, or hang out at the bars there. I was a terrible drunk, often belligerent, and I drove like a maniac.

My parents weren't involved very much in my life. Their philosophy was to let me live my life as long as I didn't get into trouble and got good grades. After Andover, it was easy to get good grades. I had a good aptitude in math, a 792 on my SAT, and got straight A's without much effort. Both of my parents were very intelligent and accomplished leaders, so I had "good DNA." I was among the top of my class at New Canaan High. At Andover, I was barely average.

It was sports, however, that saved me from getting 100 percent out of control. Our hockey team was the first ever to go to the state finals. I was the high scorer on the team and was voted to the All-State team. I couldn't even make the varsity team at Andover, not even close. I also played on the tennis team and we won the state championship. Those activities kept me grounded, at least during the week.

When it came time for me to make a decision regarding college, however, I faced a dilemma. I didn't want to go to Yale, but without some type of intervention, that appeared to be my fate. I had the smarts, the grades, the sports, but all of that would probably not have been enough, considering the level of competition. But what I did have was that list of relatives and that made me a shoo-in. My dad helped me fill out the application. I had no idea how far back our family went at Yale, but the list of notables included politicians, judges, business leaders, etc. It was impressive, and when the Yale representative came to my home to interview me, he seemed to know who I was.

I muttered *"What?"*

That brought a slightly stunned expression to his face.

"The Yale alumni on your application, do you know how impressive this is?"

"Does that mean I will get into Yale?"

"Well, normally I can never guarantee anything," he paused, seemingly for effect, *"but you are going to Yale!"*

He spoke with enthusiasm and expected the same from me, but he was shocked by my response.

"I really don't want to go to Yale. Is there anything you can do to keep me out? If I get in and don't go, I am not sure my dad will ever talk to me again. At the very least, we will be estranged for a long time. This will follow me my whole life. I already get blamed for a lot, but this will be off the charts and unforgiveable."

We talked for quite some time. He explained the insanity of my decision and the merits of a Yale education and experience (he was probably right); and I tried to give some rationale for my state of mind. Though I couldn't pinpoint it, there was something in my soul that resisted the life of the rich and famous, that resisted the elite path.

It was really quite clear to me, though I wasn't able to put it into words. But I saw it. It was all around me. I lived in it: the cocktail parties, the country clubs, the fancy homes and interiors. It seemed everyone was striving for some kind of status and it had a flavor of hypocrisy; something about it felt increasingly artificial to me. Really, who was I to judge? I was only seventeen years old. I just knew I didn't want it. What I did want, I had no idea; I just didn't want that.

I never told anyone about my interview. And when I didn't get accepted to Yale, my dad was furious at the University, but not at me. And I could never tell him. That was one thing for which I simply would not bear the blame. Neither of us could have handled the truth very well. We all have our secrets. Right or wrong, I'm not sure.

Dropping Out

So back to Lake Forest College. I left the fraternity and I began to hang out with the "Independents," who didn't belong to any fraternity. Some were of the bohemian or artistic persuasion, forerunners of the hippies, or hangovers from the beatniks. Others were the kids that didn't seem to fit in anywhere else, retiring or somewhat socially awkward, or otherwise preoccupied; nerds maybe. Among this culture of independents, there was more of a conversation about the war. civil rights, and antiestablishment sentiments. The world was changing, and though I didn't recognize it, I was part of that change. Bob Dylan was singing, "The times they are a changin'." Our generation was cast into a remarkable set of converging circumstances and social issues. The "status quo" would never be the same again, and the student revolution would be at the center of that great societal shift.

Rebellion is not always bad. Some things need to be challenged. The minority is often right. There is something built into us that should not be quenched—something that won't always go along with the status quo. Creativity is sometimes born in rebellion. Yes, there is the well-known negative side to rebellion, but complacency in the context of abuse or exploitation is unacceptable. And if we constantly squelch in others, and within ourselves, that quality of rebellion, the results are stunting. Maybe rebellion is not the right word. Maybe we could call it *a lust for truth and justice.*

With my social network in disarray, I was playing poker almost every night from midnight to 6:00 a.m. and sleeping during the day, which meant missing classes. Once junior year hockey season was over, I was still planning on coming back for spring term and tennis season. My schedule of playing poker and missing classes interceded, and the meaning of college was fast disappearing.

During spring break, I travelled to the west coast. I went to see my sister in San Francisco; she lived on Page Street and Masonic Avenue, just two blocks from Haight-Ashbury, the notorious center of the hippie culture of America (and the world in some respects). My sister was a banker, not a hippie. She just happened to live near "the Haight." Her husband, however, did enjoy getting stoned. He and I spent a lot of time together getting high and laughing at the insanity of the world that was emerging. While I was there, a friend from New Canaan came by, Pete

Grayson. He and I were drinking buddies in New Canaan and we both switched to marijuana at about the same time. He told me Daisy and Sky, other friends from New Canaan, were coming up from Mexico (where they were going to college) to see Sky's mom, who now lived in Santa Monica, just outside of Los Angeles. Surely they would have some good grass, maybe even some of the famous Acapulco Gold. Sky's mom was always very cool about letting us hang out at the house.

So Pete and I were on our way to LA, and sure enough, Sky and Daisy were well supplied with pot. We enjoyed a few days getting stoned and listening to Sky tell stories about Mexico. Sky was a natural storyteller, and I remember well watching him sitting on his knees on the living room floor, rolling a joint and recounting amazing adventures of their travels in Mexico. They enthusiastically encouraged me to visit Mexico, and I left with the address of their apartment outside of Mexico City. I don't think I really ever expected to see them there. It was just a distant dream.

Back at Lake Forest, there was a redheaded "independent" who told me about a hippie commune that he had visited for a few days. It was my first introduction to such a thing, but I had heard that some of the Haight-Ashbury crowd were leaving San Fran and going "back to the land" by starting communes. He told me of a family who would welcome me and I took the name and address of the commune.

Quite a few weeks into the spring term at college, I hadn't been to one class. My poker playing and getting stoned was taking its toll on me. I had to either buckle down or drop out. College had lost all of its meaning, if it ever really had any. Rather than flunking every course and having that on my scholastic record, I went to all my teachers and told them my story. They gave me an "I" for Incomplete and it made my exit a little easier. I announced to my parents that I was dropping out of college. They almost seemed laissez faire about it. I'm sure they were very confused by my restlessness.

Quitting my fraternity and dropping out of college proved to be two events that would radically shape my future. Down the road I went in my Volkswagen bug, headed for the hippie commune, and the possibility of

Mexico. This moment could surely be identified as my step into real life and the journey to discover who I was.

My first stop was Saint Louis, where my grandfather had been an Episcopalian minister for twenty-five years and had a plaque there in his honor as "The champion of the underprivileged." He now lived in Pasadena, California, but perhaps some of my roots were right there in Saint Louis. They also must come from my parents, who in their own right were both great humanitarians. Mom and Dad were independent in their thinking and followed in the footsteps, philosophically, of my grandpa.

I spent just one day there visiting with people who deeply admired my grandpa. But the road was calling. The hippie commune awaited me, though it wouldn't turn out to be anything like I expected.

CHAPTER 3

MEXICO

How does it feel, to be on your own,
with no direction home,
A complete unknown, like a rolling stone

—Dylan

I found my way to New Buffalo, New Mexico, and the very same hippie commune that Peter Fonda and Dennis Hopper visited in the iconic film *Easy Rider*. There was some debate at the commune over whether to allow the filming, but for whatever reason they permitted it, and so it is forever chronicled. The commune was a group of teepees, built by the hippies who lived there. New Buffalo is mostly desert, about an hour outside of Taos. It is surrounded by beautiful mountains, but otherwise rather desolate. The hippies had come here to "get back to the land" and create Utopia. They soon discovered that a major hindrance to that aspiration was to be found in their own humanity.

The couple I stayed with lived in a small run-down house just a hundred yards down the road from the commune. They were somewhat critical of the commune for its tolerance of "wife swapping," though no one was really married. They also opposed the filming of *Easy Rider* for some moral reason that didn't make much sense to me. The husband was a self-proclaimed Buhu minister and "dropped" LSD on a regular basis. The wife was trying to be a good mother to her young children; she gave me my first introduction to a healthy diet. They were very accommodating, but there wasn't enough inspiration to keep me there. A little disillusioned, I realized they hadn't found Utopia, and I wasn't prepared to stay there until they did. After a couple of weeks, I was off to Mexico to see if I could find Sky and Daisy, about fifteen hundred miles away in a land I had never been in and whose language I didn't speak.

This was an age before Internet, computers, cell phones, or Google maps. It was, *"Get a road map, hope you can find your way and ask a lot of questions of people as you go.* Those people usually had different ideas of how to get there, and when they spoke Spanish, it became especially difficult. But down the road I went, crossing into Mexico for the first time at Ciudad Juarez, down through Chihuahua, San Luis Potosi, and on into Mexico City, at the time a city of about eight million inhabitants. How I found Sky and Daisy, I am not sure; they lived in a little apartment in a small town with dirt streets west of Mexico City named Cuajimalpa, which probably isn't so small anymore.

This was the beginning of a new chapter of my life: experiencing life in a third world country, adventures travelling all over Mexico too numerous to recount, living on my own, and discovering what was important. My first trip to Mexico lasted only three months, but it felt like a lifetime. On one excursion with Daisy and Sky, my VW broke down on the way to Acapulco and some guy with a big knife wound scar on his belly who posed as a mechanic said he could repair it. I left it with him, and along with Sky and Daisy, hopped onto the back of the local version of a commercial truck. We swallowed some "speed" (amphetamine) and raced through the curving roads lying on top of a tarpaulin that covered whatever this trucker was carrying in his trailer. I yelled over to Sky and Daisy through the noise of the truck and the wind with a little concern in my face and voice.

"Do you think we're OK?"

"I hope so," answered Sky with a forced smile.

He was the "expert," but his body language was not exactly reassuring. Regardless, we had made our choice; we were on this truck, holding on with every corner. There were hours of them. It was nighttime, frightening yet exhilarating.

We made it to Acapulco, the truck dropped us off, and with great relief we made our way to what seemed like a deserted beach a few miles outside of town. We slept on the sand. We were awakened just after dawn by a small tidal wave that broke on the beach and washed us up onto the land beyond the beach. It was unique entertainment for a few Mexicans who witnessed three gringos get transported by the wash of what must have been an enormous wave and deposited on the ground as the water receded. Welcome to Acapulco, Puesta del Sol, to be precise. After that, we rented a room in a not so fancy seaside motel.

I ended up travelling to Acapulco a number of times during my stay in Mexico. It would become the site of one of the major episodes in our smuggling experiences. It was also the source of some of the best quality marijuana in Mexico, with a well-known reputation among the young people in the States. Smoking "Acapulco Gold" was like driving a Mercedes, or eating filet mignon from Argentina.

Sky and Daisy were attending the University of the Americas (now in Puebla, then just outside of Mexico City), on the highway to Toluca. They lived together in a small apartment across the street from a mushroom factory. They allowed me to sleep on the couch, and I remember observing their relationship together. It was the first time I lived with a couple for any length of time and I was struck by observations that were new and quite educational.

Daisy was into sharing, something I never learned or observed growing up. She was very unselfish in a way, even thoughtful. I'd never seen that before. Sky was helpful around the house, sweeping and trying to keep the apartment neat. They seemed to get along quite well living together. They had been boyfriend and girlfriend since high school, but this was their first experience living together and it looked like it was going pretty well.

When the school year ended around the first of June, we headed back to the USA to find work. Money was running low, especially for Sky and Daisy. We drove up the coast and stopped to surf at San Blas, north of Mazatlan, a sleepy little fishing village famous for its surf, sandals with soles made of old tire treads, and its "No See-ums," tiny bugs that came out at sunset that were so small they could penetrate mosquito netting. I remember a friend named Dirk who decided to save the three-dollar-a-night hotel room and sleep on the beach. The next morning when we saw him, it was scary. He was covered from head to foot with red bites. Don't sleep on the beach in San Blas.

JUSTIN IN MEXICO - 1968

On to the border and back into the USA. This was my first time going through US Customs and a border inspection to reenter the United States. We carefully discarded any remains of the "Acapulco Gold" and prepared to make the crossing. We wanted no trouble with the law. Everything went quite smoothly. They searched our cars, asked us some questions, and welcomed us back to the USA. I don't believe the insane idea of smuggling marijuana across the border was even a distant thought for any of us at the time. But there was a major life change emerging that would alter everything.

CHAPTER 4

SAN FRANCISCO

Blackbird singing in the dead of night
Take these broken wings and learn to fly
All your life
You were only waiting for this moment to arise.

—Paul McCartney

We made our way to San Francisco and rented an apartment in a building known as "The Blue Palace." It was about twelve stories tall and obviously blue, but not a light or powder blue. It was a strong, vibrant BLUE. It was in the African American section of San Fran and, consequently, we were the only white people in the building. I never felt uncomfortable there, but Daisy did. It was not due to prejudice on her part; racial tensions in many inner cities across America were not uncommon at that time, though San Fran was not specifically known for them.

I really felt very at home in the Blue Palace, perhaps because I always sensed that I had a good dose of soul for a white guy, or maybe it was because I had quite a lot of interaction with black guys and girls growing up. Additionally, my bridge partner at Andover was black and from my point of view, I considered him my best friend there. We spent *a lot* of time playing cards together! No matter the reason, I felt at ease in their culture, though the feeling may not have been mutual for some of the other residents. If so, I was naive to that and just decided that I fit in. Besides, many were very friendly toward us and made an effort to help us feel accepted.

I called that summer at The Blue Palace, "The summer of Aretha." Aretha Franklin, the future Queen of Soul, had just released her second album and whites and blacks alike were embracing her voice and sound. The Blue Palace was rocking (maybe quaking would be a better word) with Aretha. It didn't matter what floor you were on, Aretha was booming out R-E-S-P-E-C-T, or "Chain of Fools," or "Think," or "Natural Woman." The volume levels of 1968 sound systems were being tested. It was "Dancing in the Street" time, except it was in the rooms and halls of the Blue Palace. The halls were roomy with high ceilings and about twenty apartments opened up on the one long hallway of each floor. So as people opened their doors and danced and partied, each floor became like an open house event. I loved it. And I fell in love with Aretha forever, like so many others. We only stayed there a month, but somehow I always felt like I knew Aretha a little better than the rest of the world because I got baptized with her at the Blue Palace. My thanks to those other tenants for accepting this twenty-one-year-old, long-haired hippie white kid into their world for a month. I felt like I never completely left. I remember Sly of Sly and the Family Stone saying to a white crowd on Ed Sullivan, "Thank you for letting us be ourselves." I felt the same way toward the brothers and sisters of the Blue Palace.

We spent the next few weeks in an apartment we rented before we found a more permanent home. It was on the second floor, just above the landlady. She was the mother of Stephen Stills of Crosby, Stills & Nash. I don't know if Stephen still lived there but we bumped into him a few times. What was even more memorable was the number of times we would hear a tap-tap-tap on our window, only to look outside and see Mrs. Stills with a broomstick hanging out her window directly below ours, banging on our window with the broomstick handle to tell us to turn down the music. It wasn't long before we got the message and moved out.

We moved into an old sea captain's house in the middle of the "Ticky-tacky houses all the same" environment of South San Francisco. It was the only remaining house on the street that wasn't one of the new boxes with a small square lawn in front. Our house, perched on top of a small hill, had boulders covered with ferns and flowers cascading down to the street. We loved it. Many times I sat on our front porch casually meditating, but with a growing conviction I spoke my mind.

"Whether I end up rich or poor, I will never settle down to boredom with a 9–5 job that I don't like and a lawn and a life that is too small."

I didn't know any of the people in those houses, or judge them for their fate. I just didn't want what I imagined that life to be. It was one of my first big life perceptions. I finally knew something about what I *didn't* want.

Daisy tried to get a job as a "bunny" in the Playboy club, but fortunately she was turned down and ended up as an exercise guru in a fitness club. Sky and I both started a business. Sky was an expert for his age at trimming and cutting down trees, so Tamarack Tree Service emerged. It was exciting in its own way, driving all over the beautiful Bay area in Sky's open Jeep, looking for homes with tree problems, knocking on doors and contracting jobs. The other business was mine, a sandal and leather shop on Haight Street and Masonic Avenue, just one block from Haight-Ashbury. To secure my first shipment of imported goods from Mexico, I drove down to San Blas and brought back a trunk full of sandals and leather goods. There was no inspection at the border. I just cruised across. But after a time the business was not going very well, and when the Hell's Angels came in and helped themselves to whatever they wanted, it marked the end of that enterprise.

The next business did not begin as something I would call a genuine business. I thought of it more as a "service." I was not the one who initially promoted it, but not because of any moral sanctity on my part. I just did not see it as a good way to make money. It was a way to afford staying stoned on a regular basis and being able to "turn on" our friends at the same time. As to the morality of the whole thing, this was my take on marijuana. It was a common viewpoint among our generation and it went like this: Alcohol was our parents' drug. And until marijuana worked its way into the younger generation in the mid-1960s, it was our drug, too.

I personally was a lousy drunk. I got obnoxious, wasn't afraid to get into a fight, treated whatever girlfriend I had poorly, and drove fast enough to kill myself and anyone with me. There were no seatbelts, and why more of us didn't end up dead is still a mystery to me today. My other friends were not much better. Some were worse. And there was always the hangover and the results of whatever damage you had done the night before, which you likely couldn't remember. But it was our culture and it was our lifestyle and our parents' lifestyle and there was no thought to change it. On to the next party.

Getting stoned was different. And to most of us, it seemed like an upgrade. Both drinking and smoking pot are social in nature, but drinking often seemed to degrade as the night went on. Whether an illusion or not, conversations when stoned seemed more introspective, thoughtful, or just plain hilarious. And forget driving fast: 30 mph!…"Oh my God, slow down man!" It seemed like everything on the road came flying right at you; distance and time perception were way out of whack. So, yes, you could still have an accident, but you'd be more likely going 20 mph than 120. Alcohol and marijuana at one level were simply two rival ways of getting high. Somehow I survived them both, "Hamdulillah" (an expression we learned in Morocco that loosely translated means "Thank God!").

An entire generation seemed to be breaking ranks from their elders and asking social, political, and life questions. There was almost an assumed unity; individuality was merging with community. The fact that almost 500,000 young people from all over the world could gather together at Woodstock and have a peaceful/joyful four days of fun and music didn't surprise us. There was an immediate connection and bond with anyone involved in this "times they are a changin'" movement. Race, culture, country, social status, it didn't matter. We were all in this thing together. We were one in a lot of things. A cultural revolution was in the making: war vs. peace, civil rights vs. prejudice, free love vs. marriage, rock music vs. "boring" music?

It appeared to us that most of the older generation was simply out of touch and on the wrong side of everything. That turned out to be true in many respects and the role of "turning on" and "tuning in" became for many of us an important generational responsibility. Or so we thought. Thus the moral dilemma of selling pot or hash didn't exist. Just the opposite. We felt it was the right thing to do. Please note that we didn't use cocaine, meth, or heroin or any of the so-called "hard drugs." They didn't fit our philosophy. We wanted society to be more thoughtful, more peaceful. We were the flower children, the love generation. Those other "heavy" drugs didn't raise moral consciousness by our rationale. Therefore, while getting stoned by any means is now off the chart of my current spiritual compass, at the time, I almost felt righteous for doing so. I never imagined the lengths to which we would go, however

Sky seemed to find sources for grass and hashish, supplying us and others who we met. As a result, we never felt financially restrained from smoking dope on a fairly regular basis. We all looked forward to hanging out in the evenings in our captain's house, rolling our own joints, listening to music, and discussing the insanity of the world we lived in. We laughed a lot because almost everything seemed a little funnier after a joint or two (or three or four). A friendship and comfort level was developing between Sky, Daisy, and me, and unbeknownst to any of us, the era of Sky and Daisy and Justin had begun. What it would mean in the future was just too far out for any of us to imagine at the time.

Meanwhile, I contacted an old girlfriend of mine from high school whose family had moved to a suburb outside of San Fran. I went to see her to possibly reignite our relationship. I quickly discovered that she was still in the world I was leaving and I was clearly on a different track.

It was perhaps the first time I took note that I had left that world forever. I was in a completely divergent culture. I never saw her again.

Some claimed that "the Haight" was in decline, but it was still a great place to be, especially Golden Gate Park. There was always something happening there and often some of the premier San Francisco or LA bands were playing. What I will never forget about Golden Gate Park was my first experience with LSD. Sky, Daisy, another friend, and I all dropped our "little green pills" together late one night. Early in the morning, just after dawn, we entered the park and came across some greenhouses. There were ornate bushes, plants, and flowers of all colors and varieties. I spoke to Daisy and Sky with enthusiasm and awe.

"Wow, look at these flowers man, look at the colors, the design. There is so much variety. Check this out man, the intricacies, the detail. This is out of sight!"

Daisy's face lit up. She knew me from high school. *"Glad to see you are taking in the moment. If you think that's far out, now smell them!*

Now Daisy had been appreciating flowers and nature her whole life, but for me I don't think I had ever even noticed a flower before, unless it was a dandelion growing on a baseball field that needed to be rooted up. I was all about sports throughout my youth (and of course drinking, girls, and partying). Nature had no place on my list. But the effects of LSD and that colorful burst of flowers and plants were stunning to say the least. It was the flower center of the park for sure, but for me it was also an awakening: the design, the colors, the variety, the intricate details seemed never ending. And she was right: wow, the smells, each one distinct, some powerful, some subtle. How blind I had been all my life, oblivious to the natural beauty that surrounded me.

It brought me to what seemed a rather obvious conclusion: if there was so much design in nature, there must be a designer of some sort. No great piece of art happened by accident, there was always an artist. And

If there was so much variety and beauty and color, that designer would need to be quite accomplished. For the first time in my young adult life, I wondered at the possibility of God, of something divine, bigger than ourselves, though the thought had little shape or connection to anything else in my life. It was, however, a very real and strong conviction that sprouted inside of me and never went away. Though LSD played some role in heightening that first spiritual experience, it played no role in the future. In fact it was just the opposite.

So my first "trip" was a good one, and I never really had a bad one except in Morocco on the sand dunes outside of Essaouira. To describe that summer in San Fran as life changing would be a gross understatement. It was Bob Dylan singing, "How does it feel, to be on your own, with no direction home?" For me it felt good. Freedom is enervating—everybody wants it and for the first time I was experiencing it.

Landmark Trip to South Carolina

For a moment, I left that world and jumped back into my parents' world. It was their twenty-fifth wedding anniversary and they flew me to a resort in South Carolina where they would celebrate it over a long Fourth of July weekend. What I didn't know was how much I had removed myself from the elite lifestyle in which I had been raised. My parents were not elite in their personal viewpoints, but they still lived and functioned within that society. And when on that first night we all sat down to dinner—the women in their fancy dresses and jewels, and the men in our blazers and ties—waited on hand and foot by an entirely African American staff, it was more than I could handle. I left in tears. My mom and I had a tender moment back in the condo where she made a valiant attempt to understand all that I was feeling.

"Mom, it's like two worlds colliding." I spoke through tears, mixed with almost angry emotion.

"What do you mean," she said tenderly?

"It's like I am facing being drafted into the war in Vietnam, involved in the civil rights movement, the student revolution, and a whole generation that is challenging the hypocritical values of the establishment and here we are at some swanky southern resort with an entire black staff waiting on us hand and foot."

"Do you not like the place we've come to?

"That's not it mom. This is not my world mom. It feels like we are on a southern plantation. What are we doing here?"

She did her best to grasp the moment. In fact, I think something resonated with her. I was not a part of their society anymore, I never would be again. I didn't judge them for who they were and how they lived. I simply would not be a part of it. I was discovering who I was, and who I wasn't. That weekend ended up being more of a landmark for me than for my parents celebration of twenty-five years. Very much like the decision I had made in college to leave my fraternity, this was a major step. Thoughts and convictions were developing in my soul that became core beliefs. I wanted to be real, to treat others as equals, and to follow peace with all people as much as possible. Though I didn't realize it, a spiritual awakening was taking shape within me.

Raquel

When I returned to San Fran and the Haight, I had a chance encounter with a great girl, Raquel. I knew Raquel at Lake Forest College and I was surprised to run into her, working in a dress shop on Haight Street. Raquel was perhaps the most beautiful young woman at Lake Forest. She was two years ahead of me and therefore completely out of my league at the time. But now she was in San Fran, her boyfriend at college gone, and I had a sandal shop on Haight St! I had a fairly easy way with girls but Raquel was a real score. She was playful, adventurous; and had a counter-culture spirit. Even Daisy approved. She was always on the lookout for the right girl for me, but most of them did not meet her "standard." I talked to Raquel about the path, the trip, the journey I was on. I couldn't tell if it resonated with her.

One night we all dropped acid together and went to the Filmore to hear The Grateful Dead. The Grateful Dead at the Filmore was like the epitome of a band experience at the time. While everyone at the Fillmore was reveling in the music, dancing, or just flowing with the joyful atmosphere that only the Dead seemed to be able to create, Raquel spoke loudly toward me so I could hear her above the sound of the music.

"You know that trip you say you're on... ?" There was a pause while she waited to see that I could hear her.

"I'd like to join you."

"I'd like that, too."

I don't know if it was the acid, but something happened that night and Raquel ended up on my wavelength and we became a couple. We all loved the Filmore: The Jefferson Airplane, Canned Heat, Sly and the Family Stone, Jimi Hendrix, and Janis Joplin. I had great friends, a beautiful girl, could it get much better? There was only one "fly in the ointment." It was the summer of 1968, the war in Vietnam was raging, and we were all eligible for the draft. Our world was about to completely change.

CHAPTER 5

GRENOBLE AND AMOS

The world would be a nicer place if everyone had the ability to love as unconditionally as a dog.

—M.K. Clinton

Raquel and I headed across country in my VW bug. Our destination was my parents' home in New Canaan. I needed to sell them on the idea of funding my next episode, studying abroad at the University of Grenoble in France. We stopped at Lake Forest College along the way and stayed with some of Raquel's friends. I think they wondered how she ended up with me…LSD and the Grateful Dead at the Fillmore? But she did and I was happy.

Coming home would sabotage the relationship, however. I think I was just too spaced out to handle so many things. On to the University of Grenoble I went…alone (but not really).

Alone I was, but I didn't really go to the university. I hated school at this point. To study what I considered meaningless information seemed a total waste of time. But to explore the world and be financed in the process seemed quite functional. So the idea of going to the university there to study French (and stay out of the draft) met with my parents approval and they agreed to foot the bill.

The reality was that I ended up skiing and playing hockey. The Winter Olympics had been hosted by Grenoble the previous year (1968). They had a brand new ice rink, but almost no one in France knew how to play hockey. This was my favorite sport and the one I was best at. I joined a team of Canadians who had been imported and hired so Grenoble (and thereby France) would have a competitive team in the European league. The Canadians were all good players, but the handful of French players were not. Any good European team like the Czechs would beat us decisively.

One of my enduring memories of the Canadian players is that when we went out visiting bars in the evening after practice, the bartenders and waiters would ignore the Canadians or pretend they could not understand them. Canadian French is spoken with a different accent, and is quite offensive to the ears of the native French. I spoke French with a heavy American accent, but they would talk to me because they recognized it was my second language; I was deserving of forgiveness. The Canadian "Patois" they would not forgive, or even recognize. And these hockey players apparently brought the French language to a new low.

"Look," I said, *"I'll come along as the translator since no one with an education can understand you."*

"Yeah, but we don't like you. Having you along ruins the atmosphere. And when the girls see you they stay away."

*"But if I don't come, the girls will stay away anyways because you can't speak French and you won't get served; then it's no alcohol **and** no girls."*

"That might be better than having to spend the whole night listening to you."

So back and forth we went. I became the translator and made fun of them constantly. They insisted they didn't really like me, but brought me along just so they could get served. I encouraged them that in time, if they paid attention, they would learn to speak French. They never did pay attention. The Canadians, with their good sense of humor, and the

French, with their pride and haughty jealousy for the ""purity of their language,"" provided a great mix, and many raucous nights.

As for the skiing, it was spectacular. My favorite spot was Alpe d'Huez, close to Grenoble. Most of the weekend skiers were students, like me, and apparently could not afford any car other than the odd looking little Citroen *deux chevaux*. It was sometimes called the ugly duckling, but it was inexpensive and got about seventy-five miles to the gallon. Very light-weight, it was also light on horsepower, with only two cylinders, hence the name, deux chevaux (two horses). They would chug up the steep curving roads that led to the ski mountains. Long lines of deux chevaux going about 20 mph left no opportunity to pass. I had an old Peugeot, the *quatre cent trois* (403), but it didn't help. I had no option but to wait out the march of the penguins up the mountain.

I'll never forget my first ride up the chairlift that took me to the top of Alpe d'Huez. It might have been just another day of skiing for the French, but the view for me was stunning: snow-capped mountains for as far as the eye could see. The famous French/Swiss Alps were as "out of this world" as anything I had seen in my life. I can't think of anything more breathtaking even today. I don't know how to describe it. You would simply have to see it…awesome, just awesome! And of course, no one needed to show the French how to ski. This was the era of Jean Claude Killy, the winner of three alpine events at those 1968 Olympics and the undisputed best skier in the world.

The best part was that I paid one hundred francs (twenty US dollars) to enroll at the university, sent in my papers to my draft board in Norwalk, Connecticut and got a "2-S" deferment for the next year. I never set foot in a classroom. But I did get all of the student privileges. That included eating at the student cafeteria, which provided convenient and economical meals as well as a social network for making friends.

My sister Kaylee was also in Grenoble, living in a home with some other girls on some kind of a "year abroad" study program in connection with a US college. One of those girls, Louisa, would travel with me a year later to Mexico and attend the University of the Americas. But in

Grenoble, I rented an apartment with a California girl who I met at the university cafeteria. Gerty (a hard name for any girl to live with in that era) was my age, thin, with long blond hair, but for some reason not especially appealing to me beyond the level of friend and roommate. We never got it on sexually, which most of my Grenoble friends thought was a lie, since we were living together. We shared the expense of the apartment, both of us subsidized by money from home. She had a nice car, an MGBGT. Both she and that car would play an important role in our first caper.

Meanwhile, I was waking up to the fact that I had made a major mistake in not bringing Raquel. There were no e-mails or cell phones to call her up and apologize, so I resorted to snail mail from Grenoble. By the time she got my letter, she had gone back to San Fran and somebody named Charles had wooed her; she had become (in hippie lingo) his "old lady." I had lost her. But though "The Force" didn't exist yet, It or He still had a plan; Raquel and Charles would become good friends and a major part of our biggest deals.

Not too long after I got settled in Grenoble, Daisy and Sky arrived with two dogs, Shasta and Amos. We had planned to meet there because they were on their way to Malaga, Spain, where Daisy had enrolled in a Spanish university. Her dad was a "vet" and she had access to student loans, which allowed her the opportunity to go to college in Spain.

They located my apartment in Grenoble and greeted me with a gift that became very precious to me, a puppy named Amos. Amos's mother was Shasta, who Daisy found in a dog pound in Mexico City. She looked dirty and scraggly, but Daisy could see the story inside the cover. She took her from the pound, had her professionally bathed and brushed, and when she left the groomers, she was fluffy, and pure white; she pranced like a seasoned show dog, with what looked like a proud smile on her face. Shasta went on to have four litters of puppies, forty-five of them in all. Amos was the prize of the first litter. Shasta was a pure white combination of who knows what, but looked like a Cockapoo or a small sheepdog, or perhaps a large Maltese mix. Amos had some schnauzer in him. We guessed who the father was—a schnauzer that lived in the neighborhood of our sea captain's house in South San Francisco.

Amos was one of the greatest dogs that ever lived. I still get choked up thinking about him. I travelled around a lot and took him wherever I went: Spain, Morocco, the Balearic Islands, France, back to the States, Mexico, back to the States, back to Mexico, back to Morocco, England, across Canada, back to Morocco, Maine, Nova Scotia, etc. When I walked into a house, he would quietly find his place out of the way near where I was sitting. He didn't budge unless I did. But the moment I got up to leave, he was ready. He was smart, adaptable, adventurous, playful, loyal, and surprisingly agile. He was the only dog I ever called my own. He will ever be in my heart: Amos the Conquistador of Inner Dilemmas (ACID).

Sky, Daisy and Shasta headed off to the Costa del Sol and we arranged to meet them there after hockey and ski season. I always marvel, thinking back, how we found each other without today's technology, but we always did. In a way, it was more fun, or at least more challenging. It required asking a lot of questions of a lot of people, but with persistence, creativity and intuition we would always find our way.

I made some good friends in Grenoble and collected some lifelong memories. Angelo Benito and I met there and I took a hike into the Alps with him and two Frenchmen near Mont Blanc. What started out as a beautiful, sunshiny spring day ended in a blizzard that almost took our lives. The snow was so thick that we could see nothing. We kept on trudging through the snow in the direction of a supposed cabin. And night was now upon us. The thought of dying in the French Alps did not seem romantic at all. I was young and strong, but the storm was fierce. And who were these Frenchmen anyway? The saga ended with one of the French guys finding the cabin they were looking for at the bottom of some valley. It was snowing so hard and it was so dark that we couldn't see the cabin until we almost touched it. Finding a cabin at night in a blizzard in the Alps is like finding a needle in a haystack, but an even worse situation because it was life threatening.

That night the blizzard blew past and the sky cleared. We all took our clothes off and ran to the middle of what might have been a snow-covered lake. Why we felt that we had to run out there naked I'm not sure, but it did cause us all to laugh when it was over. Freezing, but exhilarated, we couldn't help but stop and look up. I don't think I've ever seen a sky so full of stars and I've been to plenty of places where there was no light from nearby cities to dim the more distant orbs. I had travelled from the flowers of Golden Gate Park to the view of the Alps at the top of Alpe d'Huez, and now to the starry heavens near Mont Blanc, and this time there were no drugs involved, just God's handiwork. It was stunning. Two naked Frenchmen and two naked Americans, standing there looking up: we knew we'd been "rescued" by something and we were all struck with awe. They say there are no atheists in foxholes and sinking ships. I might add this night to that saying. There are no atheists among naked French/Americans looking up to the starry heavens in the middle of a snow-covered lake after having been "rescued" in the mountains near Mont Blanc.

Spring was upon us. Skiing and ice hockey were over. Amos and Gerty and I packed up and headed to Malaga, looking for some sunshine. Though it was springtime, the Costa del Sol was more like the "Costa del Lluvia" (the rainy coast). When we found Sky and Daisy they were longing for warmth as well. We met some young travelers who told us about Morocco and we were soon on the boat from the Spanish coastal town of Algeceiras to the North African city of Tangiers. Nothing in our wildest dreams could have prepared us for what lie ahead.

CHAPTER 6

MOROCCO

"Would you tell me, please, which
way I ought to go from here?"
"That depends a good deal on
where you want to get to. "
"I don't much care where—"
"Then it doesn't matter which way you go. "

—Lewis Carroll, Alice in Wonderland

It seems to me that if the Divine exists, He designed us for adventure. It is built into our nature. It is part of who we are and brings us a certain kind of pleasure and satisfaction, often quite exhilarating. The desire to explore places, ideas, or cultures, and the desire to push ourselves to the limits, to accomplish or discover or experience is an important aspect of our existence. Like a cheetah is designed for speed, so we were created to explore. Think of the vastness of the Universe. It is beyond our ability to investigate and experience in its entirely, however long we might live. And yet we step into it with gusto. That's how much adventure is built into us.

Morocco was to be a great source of adventure. I've always been comfortable with other cultures, different races and nationalities. Perhaps it was my parents being liberal democrats in a strong republican town, or maybe it was having Mexican or African American housekeepers who I spent more time with than my parents. Or maybe it was my grandpa, who I admired and respected. But in some ways I had a preference for other cultures, though my friends were mostly white Americans. Stepping off the boat in Tangiers, Morocco, was like stepping onto a different planet. There were almost no westerners; almost no one dressed in western clothes. The men were nearly all wearing *djellabas* (pronounced jellaba), loose-fitting, hooded robes that extended nearly to the ground and were not gathered at the waist. Many were made of wool and were different shades of brown. They had a monkish flair to them. Some of the women wore colored djellabas, covered from head to foot. Others were bundled and swaddled in a variety of fabrics, styles, and colors, sometimes white. The wearers of these fascinating garments were all Arabs: some black, some brown, but none white Caucasians. We were the strangers, and we felt it immediately.

The streets were bustling, not with cars, but with people and bicycles and carts and street vendors and beggars and animals. There were boys navigating the crowded narrow streets carrying boards with newly baked loaves of bread on their heads. They clasped their hands behind their backs and hunched over like speed skaters, zigzagging through the tightest gaggles of humanity without ever dropping a loaf. The colors were incredible: fruits and vegetables, rugs and blankets, spices and jewelry, clothes, signs, and artifacts. And it was all right out on the street, so close it was difficult not to brush up against the merchandise as you squeezed through from place to place. And everywhere there were eyes, dark beautiful eyes of both men and women, darting to and fro, recording everything in the environment, assessing the business of the day, looking for every opportunity.

We were immediately surrounded by young men bubbling enthusiastically, offering to supply our every need (and always for a price). Were we looking for a hotel? Did we need to find a place to eat? "Hey monn, do you want to buy this shirt, this trinket?" They were all named Absalom, Mustafa, or Mohammed. One young man named Mustafa, about fourteen years old I would guess, led us to a hotel and our life in Morocco began.

We each immediately bought a djellaba to blend in, and because it's such a practical piece of clothing for the lifestyle there. With their long blond hair, Daisy and Gerty stood out like sore thumbs, catching the eye of every Arab young man not used to seeing a woman at all unless completely covered. Sky and I wore long hair and beards, attracting every young local drug peddler on the block. They sold *kief,* the Moroccan word for marijuana, or *hashish,* the pressed pollen of the kief plant that was smoked mostly in long-stemmed wooden pipes with little clay bowls. The stuff was everywhere. Although technically illegal, it was smoked publically in a semiprivate way, meaning don't do it in front of a cop, but don't worry about it much, either. So getting introduced to the drug culture in Morocco was quick and easy and we soon moved away from our young Mustafa to discover our own contacts and friends. There were a few western hippie types mingled in the crowd that had already learned the ropes of Tangiers. We tended to hook up with them, feeling we could trust them more than the average Moroccan street hawker.

First Import

Sky came up with a bright idea. He was practical with his hands and skilled with tools (maybe shop class back in high school was worth something after all). Probably thinking about how to survive financially in our adventurous lifestyle, he approached me with a plan.

We had met a man named Absalom. He lived in a small concrete block home that felt warm and comfy inside due to colorful and comfortable low Moroccan style couches to sit or lie on, and nice quality straw mats covering the dirt floor and decorating the walls. His home was outside of Tangiers, about a twenty-minute walk into the country and we often went there to smoke hashish, drink Moroccan tea, and eat tagine, a Moroccan stew. We would sit around a small low table, either on the low couches or on a pillow on the floor, and pass the pipe while Absalom's wife would serve us tea and then later, tagine. Moroccan bread is round and delicious, baked in a wood heated oven. You tear the loaf into pieces, dip them into the tagine, and savor it as you masticate. Concurrently, you pass the pipe, which is constantly refilled and enjoy a wonderful Moroccan night without a lot of conversation, but enough to know everyone is happy to be there. We did this a few times over a period of time and became friends of a sort. Absalom was a warm, kind, simple man in his midthirties with a wife and young children. He had connections to people who grew kief and made hashish up in the hills not far from Tangiers.

Sky approached with a question. *"What do you think about the idea of concealing some hash in the spare tire cover of Gerty's car when she heads back to the US?"*

I still had some money, enough to buy about eight kilos of "hash." I agreed to the idea, and unbeknownst to any of us, our import business had been launched. I don't know what it cost Absalom, but it cost us about two hundred dollars a kilo. I negotiated with Absalom to give him half down and to trust us for the balance upon our return.

Gerty had an almost new MGBGT hatchback. Beneath the carpet in the rear was a wooden door that lifted up to access the spare tire and some tools. The idea was to replace that door with another wooden door that had a hollow core and place the hash in air tight plastic bags in the hollow space. Gerty was willing. Sky was a good craftsman and took his time to form all the joints with a perfect fit. All he had were hand tools, but Sky was patient and had an eye for quality. When it was all done, it looked just like the original wooden hatch door to the spare tire. We managed to carefully stuff it full with all eight kilos of hash. As the mathematician, I was pleased to see my calculation of space was accurate. So were Sky and Daisy. Gerty approved of the workmanship and was crazy enough to drive her car by herself from Morocco to Lisbon and take a Yugoslavian freighter called the *Yugolinea* with her car on board to the port of New York. Sky, Daisy, and I toured Morocco for another three weeks and awaited Gerty's message that all was in order for us to return to the USA, sell the hash, and share the proceeds.

And tour we did: down to Marrakech, a city made famous by the Crosby, Stills & Nash song "Marrakesh Express," then on to Essaouira, where we rented a small apartment from a wonderful woman named Fatima and discovered a man who made the best vanilla yogurt ever. I had my only relatively "bad trip" on acid on the expansive sand dunes of Essaouira, thinking we were all going blind watching the sunset.

Then we drove further south toward Agadir, the last city of any size before the Sahara. All the while I was reading Tolkien's trilogy, *The Lord of the Rings*. It became my "Bible," so to speak, in that I carried it with me and read it regularly. First of all, Morocco seemed a lot like Hobbit land and our adventure would more and more resemble what Sam and Frodo experience. And then there was the Gandalf factor, the friendly Tracker. I read and reread the book for the next two years.

We stopped at a beach just north of Agadir called Taghazout. When we arrived at Taghazout, there were eight people camped there. The beach was about three miles long with plenty of little nooks and crannies on a ridge just a hundred yards above the beach. There was one little grass hut-style beach bar run by a man named Mohammed. It had a well by it to wash clothes and get fresh water for those on an extended visit. We parked our vehicles, camped a few days and fell in love with the place. But we had a designated time and place for Gerty to contact us, and it was time for us to leave and head back to Tangiers. So we said good-bye to Taghazout, headed north, and hoped to return some time in the future.

Second Import

When we arrived in Tangiers, there was no message from Gerty. We waited a few more days. It turned into a week. Each day painfully lacked a message of her safe arrival and successful mission. The deduction became obvious; she had betrayed us and taken off with the hash. "Plan B" was quickly formulated. Sky would build a wooden dog cage for Shasta following the same construction as the wooden door in Gerty's car. It had a hollow space in the floor, ceiling, and walls that would be filled with hash. Once again I made the calculations and surprisingly it came out to the same eight kilos. We bought the hash through Absalom with the same terms as before, and once again Sky used Absalom's tools to build the dog cage over a period of a few days, at which point it was ready to be stuffed with the eight kilos as planned. Sky glued the false edges into place and when it was finished and painted black to reduce visibility, it looked quite professional. Sky had good reason to flash a mischievous glint of pride in his eye because of it.

The plan was to travel to Formentera, the smallest and most undeveloped of the Balearic Islands. Someone had told us about its beautiful beaches, cheap living, and relaxed atmosphere, so before returning to the United States, we had one more adventure. But the plan changed once again when a girl caught my eye.

We called her "the deer." There were only a few places in Tangiers where people hung out to drink Moroccan tea and "people gaze." The one we frequented most was in a bustling section of town with little cafes and shops arranged in a tight little village square. Wherever young people were staying or passing through, Tangiers or Marrakech or Essaouira, there was always a square in town and everyone sooner or later gravitated to it. Well, this beautiful tall hippie girl showed up at the square several times over the course of a few days with her friends and I was captivated by her. I discovered where she and her friends were going next.

"I'm chasing the deer," I announced to Sky and Daisy.

Daisy was my advisor when it came to girls and she didn't nix my plan of pursuit. So off I was, chasing after the deer, while Daisy and Sky headed to the island of Formentera with Shasta and the dog cage. I would meet them there "sometime."

At one point along the way I had dumped my car and bought a Triumph 250 motorcycle. I loved motorcycles and all I can remember is that somebody was heading home and needed to sell his bike. I bought it cheap, though it was practically new. Amos proved to be a great biker. He would lie down behind me on my backpack or climb in front on my lap and put his feet on the gas tank. He loved to put his face into the wind, his ears flying backward. He seemed to smile in the process. I should have bought him some goggles. He definitely had that snoopy look and he never fell off. We were quite a sight motoring down the roads of Morocco in search of adventure and romance.

I followed the deer to a beautiful mountain village with a rushing river running through it. We all camped near the river and the only reward I got was to enjoy some beautiful, peaceful time as well as watching the deer sunbathe topless along the side of the river. Other than that no chemistry developed between us. Either it just wasn't part of the flow or I was just too shy to make any aggressive moves. So it was back on the motorcycle with Amos, back to Tangiers and back on the boat to Spain. The idea was to drive up to Alicante where the boat left for the island of Ibiza and then on to Formentera. Sickness struck me down, however, and I almost died on the Rock of Gibraltar.

CHAPTER 7

GIBRALTAR AND FORMENTERA

Being soaked alone is cold.
Being soaked with your best friends is an adventure

—E. W. Smith

I think it was the water. Just after leaving the beach at Taghazout we ventured south to the desert town of Goulamine. This is where the "blue men" lived, so named because almost all of the men wore blue djellabas. It was also famous for amber stones, formed into asymmetrical beads, and herds of camels.

Herb was a hippie living alone in a tent and happy to receive some young western visitors. He became known to us forever as Herb of Goulamine, not too creative a nickname, but one we never forgot. The Westerners were few and far between and they tended to stand out. Herb was very tall, especially next to the blue men, who were mostly small, increasing his visibility. We ate and smoked with Herb in his tent, shared stories, spent the night, and moved on.

I might have forgotten Herb, except I think his water or something else that we shared that night in his tent was probably the source of my hepatitis. All I know for sure was I started to throw up and feel very, very sick. As I landed in Spain, I had the singularly inspired thought to go to Gibraltar in hopes that it would have an English hospital. It did, but it was more third world than British. It was old, dark, and generally tired looking, more in keeping with what you might expect in India than on Gibraltar. Unbeknownst to me, they gave me a bed in the death ward. Maybe it was the only bed they had, but whatever the reason, after a few days I felt like I was getting worse. No doctor ever came to see me, the food they gave me was greasy, with no fruit or vegetables, and I determined I needed to escape. I looked at myself in the mirror and it was scary. I was gaunt and my eyes and skin were very jaundiced. I weakly made my way down the hall, out of that section of the hospital, and down another hall past what might have been the front desk. A nurse abruptly halted me with a strong voice:

"Where are you going?" she demanded.

"I need to get out of here. I am not getting better, I am getting worse. I feel like I'm dying right here in your hospital!"

My jaundice skin and the desperation in my voice captured her attention.

"Where is your room?" she queried.

"All the way down this hall and then all the way down to the left," I replied.

That's when I found out I was in the section of the hospital where people were dying. She forced me back to my room with promises of better food and care, a promise which she fulfilled. About a week of fruit and vegetables and medication of some sort put me back on my motorcycle with Amos, headed to Formentera. I wasn't healthy yet, but the hope of Daisy's cooking and sunshine and fresh air and friends inspired me to push on.

It was always an adventure, the process of finding each other in these out of the way places with no cell phones and no way of making contact but word of mouth. Upon arrival in Formentera, I got off the boat, made my way to the town square and asked the question to the first person who looked like they might know.

"Have you seen a young American couple…a bearded guy with a blond-haired girl and a white shaggy dog?"

I think it was the shaggy white dog that gave the best clue. After a few people asked a few other people, someone thought they had a pretty good idea.

"I think they are renting an old stone house down this road about three kilometers."

It wasn't Google Maps, but they drew a pretty good sketch of where it was and soon my Triumph, Amos, and I found them. They said I looked terrible, which I did, but it was the beginning of a few weeks of sunshine, beaches, swimming, and healthy food. Healing followed naturally.

Three major events took place while on Formentera. On July 16, Daisy turned the magic age of twenty-one. Daisy's birthday was one of those days I'll never forget, a picture perfect day at the beach with the ocean on one side and a lake on the other. Daisy was radiant and Sky was a happy man. I was glad to share the day with them and the event. It was a little surreal—as close to perfect as a day gets.

On July 20, we looked up at what I remember to be an almost full moon and realized a man was walking on it. Even though Formentara was primitive (no cars, no televisions, not much electricity, and no phones) the news of the man on the moon travelled as fast as the Internet. It was an unusual feeling to look up and realize there really was a man on the moon while at the same time be living in extreme simplicity, completely void of technology. The awe was two-sided, but I preferred Formentera to the moon landing, if you know what I mean.

And third, we met the Zaneys. They were a book in themselves. But let me give you a few of the highlights. Zaney...yes that really was their last name, and fittingly so. Kyle and Dahlia had three Zaney children, Mack, Marcelo, and Sofia, aged twenty-two, twenty, and fifteen respectively. Kyle and Dahlia fled Texas due to some kind of southern family feud. They escaped in their thirty-two foot trimaran, sailing across the Atlantic ocean, eventually landing on the island of Formentera. Mack seemed half normal (probably just a mirage). He was almost clean-cut, fair skinned, and with a faint Texas drawl. Marcelo was long-haired, more Spanish-looking than American, and a very talented guitar player with intense eyes. He had a kind, gentle female companion named Charlotte. Sofia had taken LSD at a very young age and was wild, beautiful, and much to my chagrin, had a British boyfriend. I would later pursue her with some success in Mexico.

The whole family was musical, full of life and adventure, fun to be with...and crazy. They were followers of some Eastern guru. As for their diet, they were vegetarians. That was our first meaningful introduction to the vegetarian concept, and I wondered what one would eat. It seemed that dinner might be reduced to spaghetti and meatballs without even the meatballs! But they were so charismatic as a family, so unlike anyone that we had ever met, that their spiritual journey became attractive to us at some level. We tried vegetarianism, and Dahlia and Sofia demonstrated some creative cooking that cured us of the fear of boring, tasteless food. Daisy got on board quickly and was a natural, enthusiastic about healthful cooking and preferring to love and care for animals rather than eat them. We talked with great interest about their guru and their spiritual journey. It was definitely a shot in the arm toward exploring the deeper meaning of life.

Formentera was magical. There were virtually no cars. There was no ferry service that allowed or transported them. Everyone got around on foot, bikes, and motorbikes. I had my motorcycle. The island was narrow and only twelve miles long. The beaches were beautiful white sand with few tourists of any sort. No resorts existed on the island, as there was hardly any electricity. The house Daisy and Sky rented was typical. It had no electricity, no indoor plumbing, and no running water. A well and an outhouse were outside. There were many special days of peace and sunshine with relaxing evenings in town around the square or at home. And our friendship with the Zaneys would cross continents…which is exactly what we had to do. It was time to head home to the USA. The trip home for Sky and Daisy would be the most frightening of their lives.

CHAPTER 8

FRENCH DRIVERS AND HURRICANES

All journeys have secret destinations of which the traveler is unaware.

—Martin Buber

Sky and Daisy took the same Yugoslavian freighter Gerty had taken back to the States from Lisbon (the *Yugolinea*), carrying their dog and dog cage with them. I rode my bike back up to Grenoble, picked up some things I'd left there, sold the bike and flew home. To accomplish this, we said good-bye to our magical island of Formentera, took the ferry to Ibiza, and then back to Alicante, where we parted ways.

It was my first motorcycle ride on French roads, and it would spark another life changing event. The first day was rather uneventful; Amos was in full glory with his face into the wind most of the time. But when I crossed into France on the second day, the French motorists treated me as though I did not exist. On three separate occasions they ran me right off the road. These were all two lane roads with dirt or gravel shoulders at best. Three times I was forced onto the soft shoulder at about 60 mph and almost flipped my motorcycle as my front tire hit the unstable surface. The last time I stopped, turned off my bike, sat there for a few moments and made one of those foxhole promises. "God, if you get me through this day alive, I will never own a motorcycle again." That was a big promise for me, but I felt my life was at stake and this was my way of dealing with it. We drove to Grenoble without further incident. Amos seemed as relieved as I was, and I never owned a motorcycle again.

I flew to New York and made my way home to my parents' house in New Canaan. Sky and Daisy were due to arrive any day, hopefully without catastrophe. But catastrophe struck, in a manner that was worse than any of us expected.

What could be worse than getting busted at the border with eight kilos of hash in the walls of your dog cage? Not much, except drowning at sea under the waves of a hurricane. Yes, Daisy and Sky were on the *Yugolinea* freighter that sailed right into the middle of a hurricane. Apparently, the existing radar misread the storm's path and they hit the hurricane dead center. There were many seaman on that ship that had never been in a storm that severe. The sea was getting rough and Daisy and Sky were at dinner with the crew. It was not a passenger ship, per se, and thus they all ate together. There were only eight passengers. Suddenly, the whole dining room shifted and the tables from one side were thrown toward the tables on the other side of the room. The captain stood up abruptly and spoke with urgency and a commanding voice.

"Everyone to their quarters and crew to their stations!"

For eight hours, Sky and Daisy braced themselves in their secured bunk while watching through the one porthole in the room. One moment the porthole would be under water, and they would be looking down toward the bottom of the sea, straining their muscles to keep from falling from the bunk. The next moment they would be on their backs looking up into the sky. Back and forth they rolled, certain they were going to capsize.

The *Yugolinea* was not a new freighter. In fact, it looked old, and it strained and creaked under the pressure. People were moaning and occasionally screaming. One crew member broke his leg, and the captain broke his arm. But the storm passed and they made it to port in New York City.

Daisy today still avoids thinking about that frightening experience, the most harrowing of her life. It is hard to imagine eight hours of rising to the top of huge waves then thrusting down into the trough below and never knowing whether it would be your last plunge between the waves. There was no getting used to it, only fear and hope. But hope prevailed and apparently the Divine had plans for them other than the ocean floor. Life would go on.

Maybe the hurricane helped Sky and Daisy go through customs a little more relaxed than normal. After that brush with death, nothing seemed nerve-racking by comparison. Daisy was always a distraction for customs officials with her long blond hair, slender curvaceous body, warm outgoing personality, and, it being summertime, dressed in a way that it was hard not to notice. They cruised through customs and soon we were all listening to Sky tell stories of the hurricane, which always sounded better after dipping into a few pipe bowls of hashish.

But tracking down Gerty was on our minds. California here we come.

CHAPTER 9

GERTY, RETURN TO THE U OF A, AND THE WAR

Imagine there's no countries, it isn't hard to do
Nothing to kill or die for, and no religion too
Imagine all the people, living life in peace

—John Lennon

We sold the hash and made our way to the west coast to track down Gerty, see Ma Kindly (Sky's mom), and prepare to return to Mexico. With a little effort, we found Gerty at her parents' home in a wealthy suburb outside of San Francisco. We were hopeful to get something back from our investment and find out what happened. We knocked on the door, a little nervous about what would meet us on the other side. When the door opened, there stood before us a pale, sickly, almost pathetic looking, strung out Gerty. If her plan was to gain our sympathies, it worked. We felt sorry for her. We almost politely asked for the money back and she told us some sob story of some guy she met on the *Yugolinea* and how she blew it all with him on a short fling. We didn't demand anything from her, although I'm sure we could have used some reasonable pressure to get something for our efforts.

I guess it was the "go with the flow" philosophy that prevailed. At the same time, we learned a valuable lesson. We were way too trusting, naïve really. Not everyone who posed as a hippie was on the same wavelength. We had a moral code. We didn't believe in ripping people off—that's bad karma. And what goes around comes around. We were not driven by the money; primarily, we felt a purpose in turning on the world. We would be much more careful who we chose to work with us in the future. And we would never let the goods out of our sight again. We left with some closure, but empty-handed.

JUSTIN AND HIS FIRST VW BUS – FALL OF 1969

The money we made from the contents of the dog cage financed Sky and Daisy's next year at the University of the Americas in Mexico City. Sky and I both needed another year of college because it was our last year with a "2-S" deferment. At the time, the United States military gave you five years to finish college and then you were prime draft material for the Armed Services. The escalation of the war meant that almost every young man was going to war if he was healthy and not exempt for some solid reason. We had this last year before we would be forced to make a decision, which in large measure had already been made.

It wasn't like we were against the military on general principle, or even afraid to die while serving our country. But the war made no sense to us, along with an increasing number of American citizens of all ages. No one could really come up with a compelling argument as to why we were there. It seemed to be a war to resist, rather than support, to march against rather than join in.

As a generation, I still believe we got that right, but looking back, I think we made one big error in our antiwar movement. We should have focused our attention more uniquely against the formulators and profiteers of the war policy rather than against the common (and often drafted) soldier. The soldiers (especially those drafted) were most often innocent victims of the war machine, many of whose motives reflected an admirable patriotic purpose. But so many of us showed them little or no respect even when they returned home injured or maimed. We held them responsible for having gone to war. I feel that was a terribly mistaken by-product of our zeal to end the war. It's a nice idea to believe that if no one enlisted to go to war there wouldn't be any war. But the truth is, that is an impractical and unrealistic solution. To all the Vietnam War vets, we owe you a deep apology. Thank you for your service.

I remember the words of Mohammed Ali. He asked why he should go fight against the Vietnamese. He had nothing against them and as far as he knew, they had nothing against him. "I ain't got no quarrel with them Viet Cong, no Viet Cong ever called me 'nigger.'" Those few words said a lot about the confusing purpose of the war and the racial tensions at home. I'm sure a much more exhaustive reasoning could be set forth, but Ali had a way of making brief statements that often made a lot of sense, with more depth than people gave them credit for at the time.

It was also the year of the first draft lottery. This was an attempt to be fair regarding who was drafted. Many of us with more privileged backgrounds found ways to legally avoid the draft through family influence and milking the system. The lottery was initiated to eliminate that advantage. They took all of the birthdays and mixed them up in a shoe box (yes they really did that). Then they were put into a drum, mixed up again and drawn out one at a time. In brief, if your birthday was one of the first 120 dates drawn and you were born between 1945 and 1950, you were going to war. You would be drafted. If your birthday was drawn between 121 and 240, then you might be drafted. If you were 240 or above, you could celebrate; you were safe (unless you cared to enlist).

Like the Kennedy assassination in November of 1963, almost every young man of the proper age remembers where he was on that day, December 1, 1969. Sky and I were in the cafeteria at the University of the Americas. The morning paper had arrived and the dates were listed on the front page. A large group of us gathered around the paper spread out on a table, searching for our birthdays. I was number twenty; dead meat. Sky's birthday was number fifty-four; he was a goner, too. 2-S deferments would no longer be issued. We could live out that college year and then we were on our way to war.

For that last taste of the University of the Americas, my financing would come from my parents, but not before a visit with my grandfather, the Episcopalian minister who lived in Pasadena, California, near Los Angeles. My parents were worried about me and probably wondering whether they should continue to assist me or leave me on my own. They encouraged me during a phone call home to go see "Grandpa" since I mentioned I would be in LA. I admired my grandfather. He was one of those people that most everyone spoke well of. My dad held him in the highest regard and my infrequent encounters with him growing up were always pleasant and warm. He was both godly and cheerful, a dedicated humanitarian and a loving husband, not much to find fault with.

We talked for a few hours that evening and neither of us were bored. He was highly attentive and seemed genuinely interested in my travels as well as my philosophical and spiritual observations. We talked about the failures of religion, which he readily admitted. We talked about the civil rights movement. My grandpa was a strong supporter, way ahead of the times. He had been a friend, supporter, and campaigner for those termed "colored," "Negro," "black," or "African American" (depending on your era). That was in Saint Louis, and long before it was acceptable to live those convictions. We talked about the war, which he was totally against. He understood my dilemma as a draft-age young man. He didn't say a great deal, as I was doing most of the talking. What he did say stuck with me, especially when I finally asked him a pointed question. I had been rattling on about eastern religion and the hypocrisy of western religion (meaning Christianity to me) when I finally gave him a chance to speak. I asked about his faith and why he would follow Christ instead of Buddha.

"For me Jesus fulfills who I understand God to be."

"How so?"

"Sometimes the way a leader is personified can speak volumes. It's not everything, but it can say a lot."

"Go on."

He seemed almost reluctant to do so.

"Buddha, when characterized, is normally shown sitting with his legs tucked and crossed. Jesus is seen standing, with his arms open and outstretched to the people..."

My grandpa had lived his life in service to others, especially to the less fortunate and society's outcasts. He was active, standing, his arms open, ready to embrace and ready to serve. He had nothing against Buddha, even admired him, but felt reaching out to others in service was his calling. I will never forget him. I love you grandpa.

I had enticed Louisa, the American exchange student I had met in Grenoble, to join me and go to school at the University of the Americas. Surprisingly, she decided to take the leap. Daisy didn't get a chance to give her the good housekeeping seal of approval as I just picked her up at the airport in Los Angeles and we were on our way. Sky and Daisy still travelled in Sky's dark blue Jeep and I bought a 1962 blue and white Volkswagen bus. The VW bus was the most popular hippie vehicle and was really a van with windows and outfitted as a camper. One could travel in it and live in it; and it was economical, the perfect hippie solution. We all headed down the road together from California to Mexico City, over two thousand miles on two-lane roads. We usually did it in two to three days depending on how much "No-Doz" we took.

The University of the Americas was a great place to go to school. It was only a few hundred students, of which about half of the kids were Americans who were there for some kind of adventure. I found a cool little house to rent that was quite private behind a big wall and Louisa and I tried living together. That didn't last long. I can't remember if she was as difficult to live with as I was, but I soon realized she wasn't my type. Fortunately, she hooked up with someone else and her moving out did not create a scene. I enjoyed my little nest and preferred short liaisons to more committed relationships. They seemed to involve less hassle.

There were two courses I took that I actually enjoyed at the university: one was Spanish and the other was Philosophy. I already spoke French, but I wanted to learn Spanish and I learned languages easily. That course gave me the foundation for speaking Spanish, which would become an important factor in my future life.

At Lake Forest College, I had been a math major up until my junior year. I always loved math, partially because my head was a computer for numbers, and partially because math was always very straightforward. You were given a problem and you solved it—simple enough. English and history were often very subjective without a single "right" answer— very frustrating for a mathematician! In high school I supposedly had the highest spread between my math SAT scores and my English scores: 792 and 513. Maybe that was more a statement of how poor I was in English than how good I was in math. But in any case, I didn't like to study that hard. I just found math easy. But the nature of math studies changed as I advanced and the books didn't contain as many numbers. As it bridged into more theory I began losing interest in general. I changed to economics, then sociology and then dropped out.

Our philosophy teacher was interesting and a bit eccentric, kind of like the absent-minded professor in the way he dressed and carried himself, but very real and kind. He was an American who had married a Mexican woman and together they had a large family. We noticed that every philosopher we studied ended up going nowhere with their philosophy. By the end of the course, I was motivated to ask this pleasant teacher a question.

"Why on earth are you teaching philosophy? You seem like such a genuine person. But it appears these philosophies don't provide any real answers to life!"

"That will take more than a few minutes to explain," he replied gently, with a little sparkle in his eyes. *"I have a proposal if you are interested."*

He invited Sky, Daisy, and me over to his house for dinner. After a very nice Mexican meal he proceeded to tell us of his Christian faith, which had a mystical flavor to it, and which he was not permitted to teach at the university. His spirituality, warmth, and humble lifestyle made a deep impression on us. He made no attempt to change us. That would have been somewhat out of place and at the time a rather useless endeavor. But he did sow a seed, probably without even knowing it. That seed was not so much in favor of Christianity, but in favor of spirituality. If there were any answers in life, I became inclined to believe they could be found along some sort of spiritual journey. The next big event in life was more painful than it was spiritual, however, and it almost ended this story.

CHAPTER 10

THE ACCIDENT

"Remember what Bilbo used to say: 'It's a dangerous business, Frodo, going out your door. You step onto the road, and if you don't keep your feet, there is no knowing where you might be swept off to.'"

—J.R.R. Tolkien

Christmas break was upon us and we made the long drive back up to Los Angeles and Ma Kindly's house. Two events occurred that Christmas that impacted my life indirectly. Sky was hospitalized with back problems, which meant that I would drive back to Mexico City alone. The second was that Shasta had eleven puppies by my dog (her son), Amos. I guess incest is OK with dogs as all of them turned out bright and healthy. Both Shasta and Amos were famous on campus and friends had begged us to bring them puppies from the litter when we came back from Christmas. It became my job to take four of the puppies back down to college. The significance of that otherwise trivial event would soon make itself known.

Driving with the help of too much caffeine, I was a few hundred miles north of Culiacan, Mexico in my Volkswagen bus. It was late afternoon and the puppies were wandering around loose in the bus. They made their way under my feet and while I was trying to clear them away from the pedals I must have been looking down at them too long because suddenly I heard a rumbling and realized that I was completely off the road. There were no shoulders on the two lane road to Mexico City, so I was severely tilted with no possibility of turning back up onto the highway without flipping the bus. I looked ahead of me and there was a group of medium-sized trees down in a little grove ahead on the right. I expected I would crash into one of those trees but with only a split second to make a decision, that was what I chose to do. At the same moment, the bus miraculously steered itself up to the left and back onto the highway. All I did was hold the wheel. I never steered in that direction. But back up onto the highway I went, safe and sound.

I pulled to a stop at the edge of the road to contemplate what had just happened. I didn't know who to thank, but I knew it wasn't me. The reasonable options had all signaled disaster in some form, yet there I was alive and well on the side of the road without a scratch. Some type of intervention had occurred, of that I was certain. My heart was deeply thankful for whatever power was watching over me. Unfortunately, the drive was not over and there was more drama to come.

The stress of the near accident and the unusual deliverance caused me to decide not to drive all night, but rather sleep in my VW bus on the side of the road. In the morning, I was up and driving and entered Culiacan at about 9:00 a.m. Traffic was moving at a normal speed as I approached an intersection where a policeman was directing the flow. He was waving me on, to the best of my memory; just as I entered the intersection, out of the corner of my left eye I saw a truck coming right at me. By sudden reflex I turned hard to the right, but it was too late. The truck struck me broadside just behind the driver's side door, which caused the door to fly open. I started to fall out, but held on to the steering wheel so that half of my body was hanging outside the bus. My bus crashed down onto the pavement and the force of the impact caused it to skid down the road for about a hundred and fifty feet. I looked down and saw my left leg underneath the sliding bus. In that second or two, I said to myself, "That's the end of that leg."

The Volkswagen came to a halt. Almost immediately a group of Mexican men ran to the bus, which was now lying on its side with half of my body underneath it. They lifted it back up onto its wheels. That was the first time I felt the pain. My leg was mangled and I began writhing in excruciating pain. My memory was dulled by the pain, but it didn't seem long before an ambulance arrived. I begged for anything they had to reduce the pain and they gave me something that helped. We arrived at the hospital, where they made a modest attempt to clean the wound and wrap it. It was a very poor Mexican hospital, but they started me out in a fairly comfortable bed. The people were kind, considering I was one of those long-haired hippies who were not especially popular in Mexico at the time. But most importantly, I was alive. With a difference of only a few feet the truck would have hit the driver side door and I would have been history. But things were about to get worse.

The next morning an innocent question was posed to me. Would I mind moving to another room? Someone else needed my bed. It was excruciating to move at all, but I agreed as it didn't seem to matter what bed I was in. I didn't notice it right away, but my new bed had no mattress, just a bed pad on top of springs. As an immobile patient who would be staying for almost a week, it was a decision I soon regretted. The bedsores that developed as a consequence were more painful than the crushed leg.

One godsend, however, was the policeman who was directing traffic (or NOT!) He must have been a nice person, or felt some serious guilt, or both. He came to visit me. He had been taking care of my dog Amos and ultimately I appealed to him to buy me a pair of crutches and take me to a hotel. I couldn't stand another day or night on that metal bed. It took me almost an hour to inch my way on crutches from my bed to his police car due to the intense pain from even the tiniest movement. I hadn't had anything for pain since the first day. No mattress, no pain medication, poor quality food, no wheelchair, etc. I was glad to get out of there.

I made it to the car and we were able to find a room in a cheap hotel with a decent bed. I had my first restful sleep since the accident. The policeman brought me some fresh fruit, for which I gladly paid him. The bedsores healed and my leg improved enough for me to get around a little easier. I made my first phone call. My dad had an office in Mexico City and I knew I needed help. The wound hadn't been opened and cleaned since the first day and I sensed there was trouble. Dad arranged for his office manager to meet the train I would take from Culiacan. Once again the police officer helped me slowly make my way on crutches from the hotel to the train station. Amos was close by my side at every labored step. The puppies had all been lost at the scene of the accident and my van had been totaled, of course. I said a very thankful good-bye to the policeman and good riddance to Culiacan. The conductor helped me to the sleeper car. It was the only way I could make the trip, since lying down was still the only position I could endure, especially with the movement of the train.

After the thirty-six-hour train ride, a Mr. Bradford met me in Mexico City and took me directly to a doctor that he knew and trusted. The moment of truth would reveal what was inside those bandages. When the last layer came off, Mr. Bradford's eyes bugged out.

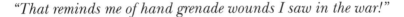

"That reminds me of hand grenade wounds I saw in the war!"

SHASTA, AMOS AND TOODY AT HOME IN MEXICO

A little gangrene had set in, but the doctor was optimistic that with time and penicillin my leg would heal. It took six months, but it did heal, though I was left with quite a scar, and my knee was never quite the same.

Sky and Daisy were already there when I arrived in Cuajimalpa after my accident. It turned out his back problems were not too serious. Daisy had a strong nurturing side to her and she was very sympathetic and helpful to my new physically impaired life. For a while, I couldn't walk without crutches, and I couldn't drive because I couldn't move my left leg easily and thus, couldn't operate the clutch of a car. It was difficult to do anything for myself for some time so Sky and Daisy would bring me groceries, Daisy would cook, and they would pick me up and take me to the university. When I got a little more mobile, I would take the local bus. I hobbled around the university and little by little life returned to almost normal, until I got a letter. Sofia and God were coming to town, which made quite an alluring combination.

CHAPTER 11

GOD IN DF

Every exit is an entry somewhere else.

—Tom Stoppard

Mexicans refer to Mexico City as "DF," short for "Districto Federal." Though normally quite warm, DF experiences a mild winter due to its five thousand foot elevation. That winter, Kyle and Dahlia and family were drawn to Mexico by the allure of warm weather, cheap living, good "grass" (marijuana), and white sand beaches. What brought them specifically to Mexico City was to visit us, and also to meet with their guru, who was coming to town to hold a "sitting." That meant two things: one, he was available for private interviews, and two, he would sit somewhere with all his devotees for a period of time. During that time they could gaze upon him, see his light, and discover that he was in fact…God. Although it all seemed a bit far-fetched, I was open to searching for spiritual life, though not at a very aggressive level. However, if God Himself was about to make a personal appearance, I considered that might be something worth taking the time to attend. There was also an additional "perk." Sofia was there, and her boyfriend was not.

The prospect of both encountering God and starting a romance with Sofia raised the fascination level from interesting to irresistible. Daisy thought Sofia was too young and unstable for me, but I felt no obligation to heed her advice on *every* occasion, even though she nearly always offered it. Sofia was simply too much to resist: free-spirited nearly to an extreme, a beautiful figure with a lovely face, and complexion that had just enough of a Latin glow to round out the aura of feminine attractiveness. She was musical and skilled in the culinary arts. She was the ideal package of a young man's dream and the lure of romantic involvement with such a mystical siren was overwhelming. After all, I was twenty-two years old!

The guru arrived and I was quite excited about my private viewing/interview and the possibility of discovering God on earth. Some seemed intimidated by the interview, but I was not. When my time came I went forward with only a modest sense of reserve. In a rather nondescript public building in downtown DF, I was escorted by a bearded Indian man into a medium-sized, comfortable room where the main attraction sat on a rather modest couch. I was expecting more—perhaps a throne of sorts or at least something ornate. The couch just didn't quite fit the occasion. The surroundings felt too normal, a nice location in a large, fairly modern city. His presence, however, did give the environment a distinct flavor. He appeared to be somewhere in his early sixties, with a big white beard and kindly face; he was the perfect image of a guru. I sat in a cushioned chair, and before long I asked him my first and most burning question. I wasn't one for wasting valuable minutes in the presence of someone supposedly divine, but I was respectful.

"So your followers say you are God. Are you?"

"What do you think?"

His question tested me. I answered him honestly, yet with some curiosity and interest.

"You look like a man to me."

He nodded with a little smile or maybe a twinkle in his eye, like you might expect from a guru. And that was that. I felt like I had my answer. It seemed he had let me in on a little secret. He was just a man.

We proceeded to a large restaurant that was entirely reserved and had been partially cleared of tables to provide ample room for another group viewing of the guru—a final opportunity to "see the light." But nothing happened there for me, either, and when the night was over we said our good-byes to Kyle, Dahlia, Sofia and family and they headed off to Merida, a cultural center of the Yucatan Peninsula, near the Mayan ruins. They left us with an invitation to come and see them, which we did, and ended up with an unexpected Robinson Crusoe experience.

CHAPTER 12

DESERT ISLAND LESSONS AND *DUMB AND DUMBER*

Not all those who wander are lost.

—J.R.R. Tolkien

When spring break came, Daisy, Sky, and I drove Sky's Jeep east across Mexico to the Yucatan Peninsula. It was an eventful little expedition. Merida was a sleepy little seaside town where Kyle and Dahlia and family were renting a house. We found a house to rent for a few days with literally nothing in it except hooks in the walls to attach your hammock to for a bed.

We soon decided on an adventure over to Cancun and the Caribbean waters. Cancun, today's Miami beach of Mexico, did not yet have a single high rise hotel, but still it was too commercial for us. We had our eyes on a little island somewhere between Cancun and the island of Cozumel. We investigated an area on the shore where fishing boats were congregating and made a deal with one of the fishermen.

"Take us out to that island and we'll pay you half. Pick us up in four days and we'll pay you the other half."

"Si senor, vamanos!"

He thought that fair enough and soon we were on our way. I wonder if it ever occurred to us that he might not come back. I guess we would have figured out something if he had deserted us, though I'm not sure what. When we got to the island it was deserted. I mean really deserted. He dropped us off at a small, not too stunning beach with coconut trees in the distance, but not much vegetation where we were. We confirmed the timing for his return and he left quickly. His little fishing boat disappeared into the distance with no land in sight, and no communication. We had a few jugs of water, some rice, beans and vegetables, sleeping bags and a couple of pots to cook and eat out of. It wasn't as if we had planned this excursion in great detail. We just did it without thinking, and there we were, marooned on a deserted island.

A DESERTED PALAPA WHERE WE HUNG OUR HAMMOCKS - 1970

We made a little campsite, lit a fire, and began to prepare some food. Dusk arrived quickly, and so did the mosquitoes. It seemed they hadn't had flesh to suck on in a long time, and they attacked us ferociously. Maybe our tropical getaway was going to turn into a nightmare. We built up the fire and added vegetation to create plenty of smoke, and then sat downwind. The smoke stung our eyes, but it repelled the mosquitoes and we found relief. When nightfall came and the food was ready, we were able to enjoy our dinner. We crashed early and slept hard.

As dawn came, we explored our island home only to discover there was no source of food or water. But there was that coconut grove on the other side of the lagoon. Necessity is the mother of invention. We would build a raft.

So Robinson Crusoe and the TV character, find-your-way-out-of-trouble star McGyver, teamed up and went to work. I had a machete. After all, we were in Mexico and every male in Mexico has a machete. There were plenty of vines and bamboo, so within two to three hours, Sky and I had constructed a small raft. It was not strong enough to hold people but seaworthy enough that we could swim along next to it and reach the coconut grove. We didn't think about sharks. We were on a mission. It took about half an hour to get there and another two hours of work in the coconut grove. We picked ripe, brown coconuts from the ground and green ones from the trees. Some of the trees were not as hard to climb as others and we could get up a few of those and cut down some green coconuts for water. If you are not familiar with coconuts, the green ones have a nice, mildly sweet water in them that is very refreshing. The brown ones have coconut meat in them that is very nourishing and quite delicious, especially when you have built a raft, floated over, climbed the trees, loaded up with more than a week's supply and floated back. And enjoy them we did...at every meal and in between meals. They made the rice delicious in the morning (rice pudding), and provided dessert at night.

Then it was fish time. Surrounded by sea, we set our mind to catch some fish. Sky was a pretty good fisherman from his youth, but all we had was a line and hooks. That proved adequate. More difficult than catching the fish was the moral debate it provoked. We had been vegetarians for over a year now and had never given much thought to where fish fit into the picture. Kyle and Dahlia preached not eating anything that has life, so for them fish was definitely off the list. Their influence had some clout with us. But then Christ ate fish, so some of the divine teachers of history seemed OK with it. We weighed the pros and cons without any real clarity.

That morning Sky was using the line he had brought which had multiple hooks on it, separated by a foot or so on the line. As he got his first bite and was excitedly reeling in his catch, the fish gave a last pull and began to run with the line. Sky did not realize that he had reeled in the line past one of the hooks and as the fish ran, the line slipped through Sky's hands and hooked him, right up in the palm of his left hand. We removed the hook with considerable pain, and released the fish. That night around the campfire Daisy started the conversation.

"I guess now we know how it feels to get hooked."

"That settles it." I interjected abruptly.

"Totally," summarized Sky. *"We leave the fish in the ocean."*

I can't say whether fish feel the same pain Sky did, but it was enough to push us over the edge. It wasn't the most scientific decision we ever made, but when you're young and trying to understand the mysteries of life, the little things, or should I say, life's little experiences, can offer wisdom in strange ways. We would have more lessons, some humorous, some striking, and many that were difficult to ignore.

Well guess what? The fisherman returned for us, we had our desert island experience and we were glad to get back to the mainland and make our way home to Mexico City and the University of the Americas.

Back at school there was an attractive blond girl who I had my eye on. I was hoping I might encounter some kind of steady girlfriend at school, but I was a little shy sometimes and often picky. Before my accident, during the fall term, I was practicing some yoga at my house and she and I had talked about spiritual life and doing yoga together there. I found her quite attractive, but she seemed a little straight, meaning she was probably from the Midwest and wasn't part of the hippie culture, at least not yet. But she was in Mexico and she was available. And as straight as I thought she was, she asked me an interesting question one day during the winter term that had also been on my mind.

"Can yoga be practiced in the nude?"

"Yes, it definitely can be," I replied rather nonchalantly as I tried to hide my surprise.

Well, it wasn't every day I got that kind of an invitation! But I did nothing to follow up on it. Nothing at all! I still couldn't bend my leg easily, but wasn't there something that could be done to accommodate such a request?

In case you haven't seen the movie, it reminds me now of *Dumb and Dumber*. At the end of the movie the two of them are walking out on the highway complaining about all of the bad luck they'd had and wishing sometime they could just "catch a break." At that very moment, a large Hawaiian Tropic bus pulls up and about twenty models lean out the windows and greet them. Then three especially luscious Hawaiian Tropic girls step out the front door of the bus and ask them if they know two "oil boys" who could accompany them on their bikini tour and lather oil on their bodies before each competition. Jeff Daniels answers that the ladies are in luck. There is a town down the road about three miles where they can surely find a couple of guys. The models look confused, as obviously they were expecting a different answer, but the door closes and the bus starts down the road. At that point, Jim Carrey says to Jeff with astonishment bordering on anger, "Do you know what you've just done?" and goes running after the bus. When he catches it, the door opens again and the models look outside the door at a gasping Jim Carrey who, catching his breath, exclaims apologetically, "You'll have to forgive my buddy, he can be pretty slow sometimes (a short pause for effect while he is still catching his breath a bit)…but that town is three miles in the other direction!" And the movie closes with Dumb saying to Dumber, "We'll catch our break someday; we'll just have to keep our eyes open." So I finished out the school year without a girlfriend of any kind, wishing I could catch a break sometime. I'd just have to keep my eyes open.

As the school year ended, I decided that before we returned to California I would take a bus to Merida to find Sofia and her family. It was about a twenty-four hour bus ride, but with air-conditioning and not too many stops it did not seem that long. When I arrived in Merida I found them without much trouble. Sofia was available and we hit it off. For a glorious few days I fell hard for Sofia, and she for me. I had to get back for the trip north, however, and Sofia still had her English boyfriend in the back of her mind and would need to settle things with him. Our plan was to reconnect in the States as soon as possible. I headed back to DF, hopeful and in love. But when I bought my ticket back to DF, I didn't pay close attention and ended up on the local bus. This time it was without air-conditioning, windows open, stops at every little Mexican village, crying children, and an array of animals. It was quite a scene. Summer in Mexico is hot and muggy and that bus was hotter and muggier. I had my twenty-third birthday riding on a crowded bus back to DF with the chickens, the roosters, and the goats. Arriving home, Sky was ready with the next scheme.

CHAPTER 13

THE THIRD IMPORT
THAT WASN'T

*Success is the ability to go from failure to
failure without losing your enthusiasm.*

—Winston Churchill

When the school year ended, money was short again. We made many friends at the University of the Americas and two of them were a couple named Tom and Molly. Tom owned an old military truck, the small, closed-top kind with big tires. The thought was to fill his tires with some Acapulco Gold, famous now among the hippie community for its color and quality. We made a contact in Acapulco, purchased about ten kilos of this high quality marijuana, and headed up the coast for the long drive back to California.

About a hundred miles before arriving at the border, we found a suitable garage and stuffed the loose marijuana into the tires. We reinflated them and headed down the road again, Tom and Maggie in their truck, Sky, Daisy, and I in the Jeep. As we reached Mexicali, the border town on the Mexican side of Calexico, California, we reconvened on the side of the road. Tom and Molly said they had smelled something strange as they had been driving. We checked the tires. The Acapulco Gold had become Acapulco Black, burned to a crisp from the heat built up inside the tires. It was nothing but ashes. Obviously, this was not our most well planned escapade, so back to the drawing board and a visit to Raquel and Charles up in San Francisco.

CHAPTER 14

ACAPULCO GOLD – THE FOURTH IMPORT

Let us step into the night and pursue that flighty temptress, adventure.

—J.K.Rowling

Charles turned out to be a fairly heavy hitter in the hippie drug culture. He was a few years older than us and well established with many good connections. We shared with him our newest idea and he wanted in on the deal. He would partially finance it for us and sell the product when it arrived. I would finance the balance. It was "all in," bigger and riskier than anything we had done so far and requiring all of our finances. How we evolved to make such a risky, life altering decision is hard to explain. The truth is we didn't really talk about it. We didn't evaluate it, we didn't do the pros and cons thing, we didn't think about it. It was the next plan and we had the resources. We just went with it. Here's the deal…

We would rent a camper, the kind that rides in the back of a large pickup truck and extends out and over the end of the pickup bed by about four feet. We (mainly Sky) would build two, four- to five-inch-high reinforced aluminum boxes that together were the exact shape of the pickup bed. We made two for easier removal and to make it easier to pack. We would then remove the camper, place the aluminum boxes in the bed of the pickup and then drop the camper back down into the pickup bed. You couldn't really tell that the box was there because the back of the camper hung out over and past the bed of the pickup. We constructed them right there at Ma Kindly's in one of the suburbs of Los Angeles. I don't know what the neighbors thought we were doing, but no one asked any questions. After about a week of metal work Sky, Daisy, and I were on our way back down the long haul from Los Angeles to Acapulco. We would meet Tom and Molly in Mexicali on a given date and they would drive the camper across the border for a thousand dollars. Tom cut his hair short and Molly could look really straight when she needed to, so they were ideal for the crossing.

Upon arrival in Acapulco, we spoke with our Mexican contact and negotiated quantity and price: one hundred kilos at forty dollars a kilo totaling four thousand dollars in cash. That may not seem like a lot of money, but in 2015 terms that's about sixty thousand dollars, which is a lot of cash to carry around and give to a drug contact in Mexico. Only a day later, we were to meet him at night down a dark dirt road about twenty miles outside of Acapulco. After a mile or so down that road, with the jungle on both sides, our contact popped out of the jungle and asked us if we had the money. We flashed him the cash and he then told us to wait. A very long ten minutes later some men showed up carrying gunny sacks full of what we hoped was marijuana. We had no way to weigh it, but our contact guaranteed it was all there and we had no interest in doubting him. We opened a couple of sacks and it looked like good Acapulco Gold, so we loaded it into the back of the camper, gave him the cash, and drove off.

The "score" had gone seamlessly, except for the fact that one hundred kilos of marijuana was much bulkier than any of us imagined. We had never seen a hundred kilos of grass before and there was no way that we could hide it in the back of the camper. If we got stopped by the Mexican police, better known as the Federales, we were toast. The Federales had an ominous appearance to them, always carried machine guns, and were never friendly. Everyone feared them, Mexicans and tourists alike. And now we faced the next and most worrisome part of our exit.

On the road, really the only road leaving Acapulco heading north toward California, there was often a checkpoint. Now that I think back on it, it would have been smart to drive ahead in a car or taxi to see if the Federales had the checkpoint set up that night. We knew it wasn't always there, but we didn't know if it was there that night or not and you can't see it until you come around a corner and there it is. But that detail hadn't entered our heads and the three of us were driving out of Acapulco with a hundred kilos of weed in the back of the camper, covered up the best we could, but easily discovered by just sticking one's head in the window. So down the dark and now ominous road we drove, around the bend to where the checkpoint usually stood.

"Look man," I exclaimed. Sky and Daisy looked.

"No checkpoint!"

And there it was…nothing…no checkpoint! I don't think any of us were breathing and we didn't even celebrate. We just drove on and on and never saw a checkpoint. Then we began to have engine troubles, not serious, but an occasional sputtering. We managed to drive eight or nine hours until we found a decent place to pull over on a side road, slept a few hours and began the next stage.

It was daylight now, so we jacked up the camper, removed the two aluminum boxes, lowered the camper back down again and brought the metal boxes into the camper and began stuffing them full of marijuana. We had a couple of "two by four" pieces of lumber to jam the "Gold" into the boxes, but this time my calculation was a little off. We had two problems: the weed was bulkier than expected, and when we really jammed it in there, the sheet metal expanded, creating bumps or hills rather than lying flat. So we sat there inside the camper for hours, surrounded by large sacks of Acapulco gold, emptying it one scoop at a time into the metal boxes. We hadn't thought ahead of time about how to empty the bags so we made do by using some of the drinking glasses provided in the camper we rented. We dipped the glass into the bag of marijuana and scooped out a glass full and dumped it into the box. Then we tamped it down with the end of the two by four and tried to get as much in as possible without creating overly exaggerated bumps. So we worked it and reworked it until it was just slightly expanded and we hoped the weight of the camper would flatten it out while we drove north to the border. In any case we had to leave about ten kilos behind, which we emptied out in the woods. We wondered whether peace and love might come to the wild pigs that are common in that part of Mexico.

When we finished packing the sheet metal floor we raised up the camper again and placed the two sheet metal boxes onto the floor of the pickup. The ends where we had been dumping the "Gold" we sealed closed with a piece of sheet metal that gave it a semifinished look. The two unfinished ends were face to face in the middle of the floor, so they could not be seen. But the edge that faced out, at the end or tail of the pickup bed was almost perfect in appearance, a very finished look as we had not needed to open that end to load the grass into the false floor. After we placed them back onto the floor of the pickup, the bumps and humps from overstuffing the marijuana into the sheet metal boxes were quite obvious; it didn't give us a feeling of satisfaction, like after a job well done. Nevertheless we went ahead and lowered the camper back down into the pickup bed and hoped the weight would flatten the boxes from the weight. It definitely was riding a little higher than we liked and looked a little awkward, but we had a lot of miles of Mexican roads ahead of us. We had a pretty good chance of seeing it flattened out by the time we arrived at the border.

Meanwhile, we had our engine problems to deal with and managed to limp into a fairly large town where there was a garage that had a Ford sign on it. The mechanic suspected worn points, which he fortunately had in stock, and we were on our way again in just a few hours with a smooth running engine and ninety kilos (two hundred pounds) of grass safely packed in our false floor. We were feeling a little better.

We made it to Mexicali on time. Tom and Molly were there looking like a couple of innocent young tourists. There was no paperwork that showed when the vehicle had come into Mexico, so they were to say they had come over for the day. They drove their truck down and we switched vehicles for the crossing. Remember, there were no drug sniffing dogs in this era of border crossing, so the risk seemed reasonable. The trip had packed the grass down as hoped and the camper was sitting nice and flat on the bed of the pickup. Tom and Molly crossed without any significant inspection and we switched vehicles again, paid them the one thousand dollars we promised them, and headed up to San Francisco. We had successfully smuggled our first substantial quantity. We never sensed the risk appropriately. We were going with the flow.

CHAPTER 15

SAN FRAN AGAIN

Oh Maggie I wish I'd never seen your face
You made a first-class fool out of me
But I'm as blind as a fool can be
You stole my heart but I love you anyway

- Rod Stewart

Charles had promised us a garage that we could back into, out of sight, to unpack the vehicle. When we arrived at his house in Sausalito, he led us to a nearby suburb. But when we backed the camper down into the garage, the door was not high enough. So in broad daylight, with the back of the camper as close to the garage as possible, we jacked the camper up, and slid the two sheet metal boxes out of the bed into the garage. Then there was a room off of the garage where Charles and his friends proceeded to unpack the boxes with some difficulty, as the grass was packed down hard from being compressed over the two thousand mile journey. They were pleased with the color and excited to experience the successful arrival. We drove the camper away while they were working on it. This was Charles's part, not ours. We were smugglers, not dealers. We were glad to clear out and not have anything in our possession except a little stash of a pound or two for personal use. We hadn't smoked even a speck of it during the trip and as we rolled the first joint and passed it around, we were glad to discover the quality was as good as the appearance.

It wasn't even twenty-four hours before Charles and his team had sold it all successfully. He gave us what he had promised, three hundred seventy five dollars per kilo. We knew we could have sold it for a lot more by the ounce, but that was not our business, and for some reason we didn't like that risk. Besides, we were rich by any of our previous standards, with about twenty-six thousand dollars after all expenses. Again, in today's language, that was almost four hundred thousand dollars.

We literally did not know what to do with all that money. Should we put it in a bank? That seemed too risky to show up with all that cash. Should we hide it under our bed? We didn't have a home of our own to find a good hiding place. Perhaps we should invest it. That seemed logical. So the three of us hippies, long-haired, big beards, headbands, beads, etc. made an appearance in the financial district in downtown San Fran and spoke to a stock broker. When he suggested we invest in some up and coming Wall Street drug company, it sounded like the right thing to do. We handed him a pile of cash and walked out the door chuckling at the irony of it. When Charles treated us to a nice dinner that night, we told him of our little outing. He was not happy. "That's the establishment man, you can't support the establishment!" We listened, and not many days later, we went back and sold our stock, taking a small loss.

We enjoyed San Francisco for a month or so, spending quite a lot of time with Charles and Raquel. We made it a habit to eat breakfast at the Trident, usually waffles with strawberries, blueberries, and bananas on top, covered with homemade yogurt and a little maple syrup to sweeten it just right. Otherwise we were at Golden Gate Park during the day and the Filmore at night, or wherever the latest bands were playing. I saw my old high school girlfriend in Sausalito, living on a houseboat with her boyfriend. They were practicing Kundalini yoga and no sex. I tried the Kundalini yoga, but it didn't work for me. I didn't try the no sex. But my next experience made me feel like I wished I had.

There was a girl who caught my eye who lived in her VW bus down near the marina in Sausalito. I'd like to call her Maggie so she would fit

Rod Stewart's song, but it was Maya. She was young, blond, attractive, and flirtatious. It didn't take many days before she invited me to her bus. Within fifteen minutes I was done, just like a man. But she wasn't and she wouldn't let me get away so easily. So after a very short recovery period we were at it again until I was really done. We talked for a few minutes, but she had somewhere she needed to go. We parted with a nice kiss and a plan to meet at a concert that night in an auditorium in San Fran.

I showed up ahead of time and she was already there talking with some friends. She completely ignored me as if she didn't even know me. She didn't speak to me or even nod to acknowledge my existence. I found out later that she had just gotten over some STD. I was her first after the fact. Somehow the parting kiss bothered me as much as anything. I'd never felt used before in life, but I got a pretty good dose that day and a chance to feel what many women have felt, perhaps even some of my past girlfriends. And I couldn't say about Maya what Rod Stewart said about Maggie. No, I *didn't* "love her anyway."

JUSTIN WITH AMOS, HANGING LOOSE - 1970

It was time to head back to New Canaan to see all our friends, along with my parents, before we headed back to Morocco. As we left San Fran, Charles let us know that he could handle anything we brought him in the future if we were inclined to do something again. I don't think it was in any of our minds at that moment, but it wouldn't be too long before we would embark on our most creative and largest scheme. We had been learning, but the next escapade would require a lot more planning and expertise.

The three of us flew east together. The only thing I remember about that flight was that Daisy had the twenty-six thousand dollars strapped to her from her stomach to her hips. It was mostly a combination of twenty-, fifty-, and hundred-dollar bills, so it was quite bulky, a little heavier than she liked, but she made it. This would be the most challenging and life changing summer of my life, at least on an emotional level.

Kirby and The Universal Life Church

Arriving home in New Canaan, we spent time with our friends and respective families. As long as the war was going on, neither Sky nor I had any legal means of avoiding the draft. Our only choices were: go for our physicals and head off to Vietnam, go to jail, or leave the country. We were too young and too immature to face such a decision, but we made the one that seemed the most logical: leave the country. It wasn't that we didn't appreciate the USA, we just felt we didn't have a choice. It was like what Muhammed Ali had said, we had no quarrel with the Viet Cong. None of us really had any idea what the war was about, so Ali's sentiment spoke volumes to us. I guess the hope was that someday it would be over and there would be amnesty or some way home.

We tried legal ways to get out of the draft. I heard about a church a year earlier that had been started by a resourceful man named Kirby Hensley: the Universal Life Church. Abbie Hoffman later wrote about him in *Steal This Book*. The church was willing to ordain you as a minister for a small fee, twenty dollars, and I thought this might keep me out of the draft for religious purposes. I had investigated the CO (conscientious objector) status back in college. But since I had no religious background of any special conviction, it was soon determined that I could not benefit from that "loophole." But becoming an ordained minister of a legally recognized church, that might have some power. I called up Kirby. I remember where I was, like one of those JFK moments. It was a phone booth just a block from the Blue Palace.

"Hello."

"Yes, I'd like to speak with Kirby Hensley."

"This is he, how may I help you?" He had a voice that sounded like the hills of Appalachia.

"I'd like to become a minister of the Universal Life Church. Is there anything I have to believe?"

Kirby's reply was prompt.

"If there are two trees in the forest, can one tree say to the other tree, 'you can't grow'?"

"Uh, no," I responded cautiously, and a little quizzically.

"Well then, send me twenty dollars and we will send you a Certificate of Ordination and you will be a minister of the Universal Life Church."

End of conversation, I hung up, not elated in any way, but sort of smiling and honored at the same time. Some might laugh at the simplicity of his comment/question. But it made more sense to me than a lot of the complicated beliefs of other more recognized denominations. I got the certificate in a week. I was one of the first one thousand ministers. Though the ordainment did not exempt me from military service, or from being drafted, it still provided a basis for a growing argument that was developing in my head against the war and for peace. Besides, I had the honor of legally performing the marriage of two couples who were good friends of ours. One of the couples was Marcelo and Charlotte, who remained married, giving me a divorce ratio that was commensurate with other ministers. I performed both ceremonies in my Moroccan djellaba, which gave me the appearance of a real life pastor or priest (though a bit Medieval). Philosophically, or spiritually, I definitely had some opinions that, in a stretch, would make me religious. Sort of.

And then I got a phone call from Sofia. She was still in Mexico. She told me she decided to go back to her English boyfriend. The news was devastating. I cried like a teenager. I didn't see anyone for one whole day and then enough of that, on with life. It's amazing how some things can seem so heavy for a day and then it's over. But the next romance came from the most unexpected direction, and it would change everything.

CHAPTER 16

DAISY

Love, like everything else in life, should be a discovery, an adventure, and like most adventures, you don't know you're having one until you are right in the middle of it.

—E. A. Bucchianeri

We were in New Canaan for about a month, enjoying the summer, enjoying our friends, and preparing to go back to Morocco. Life was filled with parties where we played music, got stoned, told stories, and enjoyed one another. There was a little cottage on my parents' property that in years past served as a home for the family nanny, as both my mom and dad worked, a rarity in those days. Mom and Dad allowed Sky and Daisy to stay there, and it made a nice little hangout for us.

Then it happened. One night we were sitting, watching TV, and passing a joint. The cottage was fairly small and there were five or six of us, so I was sitting in the back of the group and Daisy was in front of me, with Sky and the others in front of her, all watching some movie on the TV. The joint would go back and forth until consumed and then the next joint would get rolled and the night would continue. I can promise you there was no intent involved, but somewhere in the process of passing the joint up to Daisy, my hand was on her shoulders and then I began to rub her shoulders in a friendly, nonsexual way.

Daisy and I had not been friends in junior high or high school. In fact, we were high school enemies. It wasn't a love-hate relationship. It was all on the hate side. We just didn't like each other at all. She was not my type at the time (more of a nature girl) and I was definitely not her type. I was a heavy drinker in those years and had many girlfriends—not a reliable boyfriend at all. Besides, she had been with Sky since her junior year in high school and there was never an attraction between her and

DAISY AND SHASTA - 1970

me, unless maybe an anti-attraction is an attraction. Don't get me wrong; Daisy was gorgeous, with long blond hair, an athletic figure, and lots of personality and friendliness in her face and persona. We just didn't click in any romantic way. But over the last few years things had changed. We had become good friends. There was no romance imagined by either of us, not even 1 percent, but I had grown to admire her as a person, and she respected me. We saw eye-to-eye on the issues that our generation faced, my interest in health, and maybe more than anything, my quest for meaning through some kind of spirituality; all contributed to the brother-sister type relationship we had.

But it ended very abruptly that night. There was an electric response that came from both of us, simultaneously. The innocent rubbing lost its innocence and I will never forget Daisy's face as she turned her head back toward me. It spoke volumes. Her face was one of total surprise and sexual response at the same time. I don't know how long that physical and emotional exchange lasted that evening, maybe fifteen to thirty minutes off and on, but chemistry had been ignited that wouldn't die easily. The next day there were multiple opportunities for affection. In the past, it was not uncommon for us to hug occasionally; there were just never any sparks. I don't think either of us had ever imagined such a possibility. I schemed and sought after a lot of girls, but never Daisy, not even once. She was my "sister," my female advisor, and Sky's girlfriend. Besides Sky had become my best friend. We enjoyed each other, he was good to me. It all happened so fast that I didn't calculate the repercussions. Like almost everything, I didn't think through the choices that were being made. I thought it would pass, like it had with every other girl in my life. Maybe it would last a few days or weeks, but I didn't think much about it, because it wouldn't last. It just couldn't.

Well, it wasn't long before the relationship got more involved, and living in the era of the sexual revolution, we looked for an opportunity to be together, and then the next opportunity, and the next. We all went up to Nantucket, to my family's summer home, which they were nice enough to allow us to use for the month of September. Now we were living in the same house together, with a few other friends who had made the trip, and the opportunities continued. I was surprised by the continued response of Daisy and I was not resisting it at all. But at the same time, I was still in the market for a mate, as I knew that this had no future. After a short romp with Winona, who Daisy totally disapproved of, I met Jenny.

Jenny lived just a few houses down the street. That is, her family had a summer home there, and she was spending September in their home as well. In the little town of Siasconset, Nantucket, we all knew each other at some level. Many of the families came there every summer and long-term friendships developed. I've gone there every summer for over fifty years. I still see many of the same friends. They keep coming back to that magical island community. I was more familiar with Jenny's brothers because she was a year older than I was growing up. In my generation, the guys rarely dated anyone older when we were teenagers. But now I was twenty-three, it was 1970, and it meant nothing. Jenny and I connected quickly.

And suddenly, for a brief moment in time, I had two women interested in *me*, but Jenny knew nothing of Daisy. We were still carrying on secretly, as neither of us knew what to do with it. But to see Daisy actually a little jealous of Jenny began to tell me that maybe there was something more serious going on. Daisy was a woman of high morals and it was conflicting for her to be unfaithful to Sky. I think because Sky had been unfaithful to her in their past, it sort of gave her permission, but she didn't like it and it had to be resolved somehow, someday. Maybe Jenny was the answer, but Daisy wasn't ready for that yet. And neither was I, as it turned out.

I persuaded Jenny to go with me to Morocco. I flew to Paris ahead of her and made my way by train to Strasberg, Germany where I bought a 1967 maroon VW bus. I built a bed into it and drove it back to Paris. There I rendezvoused with Sky and Daisy. Soon, Jenny arrived and I picked her up at the airport. We headed down to Morocco together. But my heart was divided and it wasn't long before we were in relationship trouble. I don't think we even made it a month and by the time we arrived back on the beach at Taghazout, she was ready to return home. We were both relieved, though I am sure Jenny felt unhappy with herself for making a decision to give me and this adventure a try. I wasn't very good at handling one relationship, let alone two.

I began to contemplate a scary thought. Had I fallen in love with Daisy, who was my best friend's girl? Could this possibly work if we were good enough friends and gave each other space? In the sexual revolution, maybe anything was possible, even a healthy (or at least a functional) threesome. Regardless of whether it could work or not, I couldn't, we couldn't, hide it any longer. Daisy would talk to Sky.

I don't know exactly how that conversation went down, but Sky and I never talked about it. That was my M-O, sweep things under the rug and act as though they didn't exist. I think all three of us had the same experience. I was certainly raised that way and unbeknownst to me, I was following in my parents footsteps: ignore what you can, until you can't. We never solved a problem at home and it appeared there was no way to solve this one. So Daisy spent most nights in Sky's van and some nights in mine. And if that wasn't bad enough, it got worse.

CHAPTER 17

BIG JOHN

There is a tendency at every important but difficult crossroad to pretend that it's not really there.

—Bill McKibben

In college I played a lot of poker and often walked away with more than my share of the money. Gambling wasn't part of the hippie culture and maybe I'd just lost interest. It had been a while since I had shuffled the jacks and queens. I don't recall how it was that I found myself in a card game in this big bus parked alongside the beach. The outcome would alter our living conditions significantly.

When we first arrived at Taghazout in the spring of 1969, there were some eight people camped on the beach. Now in October of 1970 there were over a hundred who had made the beach their temporary home. Long before Facebook or the Internet, there was a word of mouth communication system among the youth generation that went around the world. There was an unwritten code of ethics to help your fellow travelers find good places to stay and to communicate wherever there was something "happening." Taghazout was fast becoming one of those places. It had been placed on the unofficial trail that many of the hippies followed around Europe and down into Morocco. About 90 percent of the campers were American and European hippies, but there were also a few older folks enjoying the beach and the cheap living. There were VW vans, people in cars with tents, and backpackers with nothing but tents, or even just makeshift lean-to shelters.

And there was one big old bus nicknamed "Big John." It was a British-built 1952 edition, thirty-two-foot Leyland Royal Tiger touring bus. Big John had seen a good bit of wear and tear over the years, but was the largest vehicle on the beach. His owner, a disc jockey from England whose radio name was "Big John," supposedly had gotten sick (hepatitis as the story goes) and sold him cheap to some Canadian campers before he left the beach in distress. The current owner was now using him to borrow money to stay in a poker game. Before the night was over, I was the proud owner of Big John. I don't remember all the details of the transaction, but the lore on the beach (persisting to this very day) was that I won Big John

BIG JOHN BEFORE RENOVATIONS ON THE BEACH IN TAGHAZOUT

fair and square in that poker game. I do remember however, the next day after the game I gave the guy an additional three hundred dollars to complete the purchase. So my guess is, it was the combination of the poker game and the three hundred dollars. The reality was that possession being nine-tenths of the law, he now belonged to us: Sky, Daisy, and me. At this point, we were beginning to hold everything in common among the three of us, like partners in a business; we were hippies who didn't want to own anything individually, and mostly like three people caught in a relationship that wouldn't work, but our love and friendship kept us working at it.

Big John was a rare windfall. He had a twelve-foot sliding sun roof with inlayed woodwork. He had tapestries on the walls between the roll up windows all around and teak wood for trim. He had been beautiful inside and out, and we spared no effort or expense to restore him to his former glory. He became the Taj Mahal of the beach.

The three of us made Big John our home. It had a simple yet complete kitchen and we arranged a gathering/living area to hang out in. It also meant less "space" between the three of us in an already difficult situation. Can you imagine the emotional stress of that on each of us? Sky was the most phlegmatic, and coped with it better than I, it seemed. Daisy loved us both and was caught in the middle, unable to decide. And I was trying to figure out whether this was possible, but quite in love and suffering from the emotional toll.

The worst part for me was dealing with the down time (so to speak). The only way Daisy could deal with it was to give her focus to one of us one at a time. So when it was Sky's time, she would have to distance herself from me and I felt discarded and abandoned. And when I felt discarded, I was emotionally unstable and angry, which made things worse. I would get blamed for my narrowness and go crazy inside because it took me back to my childhood when I was the scapegoat of the family as the only boy and middle child. It seemed I got blamed for everything and my family never resolved anything. Now I seemed to be caught in the same dilemma. No one was mature enough or experienced enough to talk things through. If we had been, who knows what would have happened? There were no easy answers. So the up and down roller coaster ride of soaring and sinking emotions sped along day after day. I wasn't a poet, but I wrote my only poem struggling with that experience. I felt like a moth, flying into a flame:

Moth flies into flame,
Into light, into pain.
Into love, into blame,
Into death, to live again

Moth flies into flame,
Hope to find her heart to gain
There a moment, feel no pain
Back to flame to die again

This went on for two years until it reached a melting point, but I am getting ahead of myself again. Our biggest project was taking shape and this one would involve a lot of moving parts.

CHAPTER 18

CHURCH AND EGGS

*Don't allow your mind to tell your heart
what to do. The mind gives up easily.*

—Paulo Coelho

Allow me to insert an important side note. Religion didn't really exist in our minds, but spirituality did, and philosophical discussions were common. It is a phenomenon of being young and coming into adulthood that leads one to be true to oneself and avoid being a hypocrite. It is often out of balance due to inexperience and naivety. At the same time genuine values are developing. "Peace" was a core belief and not destroying life was another. The Vietnam War was raging, and the effort to stay out of the draft, though not as dire an issue (we were safely out of the reach of the military), was still a concern. So I had the bright idea to make Big John an official Universal Life Church. I wrote to Kirby and submitted an application and soon thereafter it was so. Big John was a church. Though we never took it too seriously, it did provide a good reason to have people over to the bus for "services" on any day of the week, at any time of the day or night, and enjoy some music, smoke some kief or hash, and get down on the government or the war or racial injustice, subjects about which we were sure to find no disagreement. "Church" wasn't so bad after all.

We were all vegetarians of various descriptions, some serious, some out of convenience. We had been discussing whether or not eating eggs was destroying life, since they had the potential to become living beings. We had lots of time to pursue any subject, significant or insignificant. Tolerance for others' convictions (except for those in the "Establishment") was a core belief among hippies, too. For that reason I don't remember any of our philosophical musings becoming heated or intense as we smoked our joints and pipes and burned the midnight oil.

But back to the eggs. Just like the fishing event on the island near Cancun, this issue was settled by experience. I don't remember if we were discussing eggs at that very moment, but it was certainly during the time when they were an occasional topic. The Zaneys didn't eat eggs, and for them it was a spiritual decision. So, we were sitting around Big John one evening talking and smoking and probably everyone was pretty stoned when someone asked,

"Did you hear that?"

"Hear what?"

"Listen."

Everyone went silent for a few seconds and heard nothing, which of course resulted in laughter and teasing whoever it was that thought they heard something. Then the sound was heard again, the same nonresult, and the same jokes and laughter. It wasn't uncommon to think you heard something when you're stoned, so the opinions on whether or not anyone really heard anything was debated with more joking and laughter. Then a third time, but this time Daisy heard it, too, and a small search around Big John was launched, but we came up empty. At that point, we declared a time of silence, which was broken by an occasional cough from someone who took too big a drag on the pipe as it made its rounds. Then again: *tick, tick, tick* and everyone heard it. Scenes of the *Twilight Zone* or Ouija board experiences erupted into the discussion, as no one could figure out where the sound was coming from. Another search of Big John also ended up fruitless. At its next *tick*, Daisy got up, thinking she knew where the sound was coming from. She placed a small wicker basket on the little round Moroccan table in front of us. In it were eight to ten eggs she had purchased from one of the peasants who sold them, along with other local produce, on the beach every day.

"Watch those eggs and listen," said Daisy.

And sure enough the *tick, tick, tick* turned into a beak, then a head; then a chick emerged right in front of us. End of discussion, no more eggs.

That experience also caused me to write a letter to my draft board. I knew they wouldn't relate to the egg story, which I admit was not too compelling, but the principle inspired me. From time to time Moroccan peasants would pass along the beach, some tending their sheep or goats, some selling their crops or their eggs. It was frequently enough not to draw attention. We often engaged them in conversation, just to be friendly, and to practice our Arabic. By this time, we had learned enough Arabic to at least surprise them, since few Anglos took time to learn their language; they were pleased with our efforts to do so.

I remember once when a baby lamb had just been born and the shepherd allowed us to hold it in our arms. It was that experience that affected me deeply. I wrote the draft board and told them of my "church" and said very little except, "Hold a baby lamb in your arms and ask yourself if you can kill it and eat it. And since I am unable to do so, how can you ask me to take a gun and join your army and go kill somebody that I don't know and don't have anything against." I don't know if it had any effect, but about a year later, I would get a stunning piece of correspondence back from that same draft board. But I'll talk about that later on. Back to our budding project, the "big one."

CHAPTER 19

THE BIG ONE AND MAKING SURFBOARDS

Adventure, yeah. I guess that's what you
call it when everybody comes back alive.

—Mercedes Lackey

Taghazout was a hidden gem for surfing. Today it is a well-known surfing destination. None of us owned a board at the time, but we spent a lot of time in the ocean body surfing and got quite accomplished at it. One day a surfboard caught Sky's attention, stimulating his creative fascination for concealing items. As with most technological wonders, surfboards have undergone an evolutionary process in their development. The early boards were made of wood. They were heavy and difficult to maneuver. As far back as the 1950s even the lighter weight balsa wood boards had begun to be replaced by polyurethane or polystyrene cores covered with fiberglass. These cores were made by mixing chemicals together and pouring the liquid into a mold in the shape of a surfboard. The chemicals would then act on each other and expand to create a solid board.

A plan began to develop to acquire some type of a van and pack hash into the walls. We would fabricate a mold, then cover the plates of hash with plastic wrap and place them into a mold. The polystyrene solution would be poured and allowed to set. By repeating the process on the other side, the hash would be totally concealed. The resulting plates of polystyrene would then be trimmed to size to fit into the various sections of the walls of the vehicle and would simply give the appearance of insulation, installed by the manufacturer. As we discussed the details, I added up what I called the moving parts:

What kind of vehicle would we use?
Where would we get this vehicle or vehicles?
Where would it go, in the walls, ceiling, floor, or what?

Who would drive this vehicle?
Where would it leave from and where would it arrive?
How would we get it to San Fran, the route and the driver?
Where would we pack this vehicle?
Where would we do the molding?
How would we get the supplies to Morocco for the molding?
Who would be our technical supervisor?
How would we have some security during the packing stages?
How would we secure the hash?
What would be the quality of the hash?
How much hash could we conceal in the camper?
Did we have enough money for this operation?
Who would be involved outside of ourselves?
How much would we pay for each participant?
How would we find those participants?

As with any enterprise of significant dimension there is a lot of timing involved and what some people call "coincidences," or serendipitous moments. For me, it is a combination of things: decent planning and preparation, finding good people, and executing at a reasonable level of expertise. And the X factor is whether it's meant to be or not. I have found in my life that as I seek to do what's right, follow the *leading* of common sense and intuition, and listen to the voices around me that I trust, including the voice of conscience, the answers and direction will emerge. It may not come out anything like you originally imagined, or it may go very much according to the plan, but you have to listen and keep listening and follow the *leading*. "Go with the flow" was one way of saying it in those days. And if the *leading* is with you, then keep going forward, and if not, then figure out how to adjust or abandon ship. Let me tell you how this enterprise was Led.

It is perhaps an offensive idea to some that the Divine could have actually assisted us in this illegal effort, but let me explain a few things.

This is not a statement that the Divine is in favor of using hash or smuggling drugs of any kind. In fact, I am of the belief today that drugs are not necessary, nor helpful, for improving a person's spiritual awareness, developing good character, or making them a contributing human being. But in everyone's journey there are steps and stages along the way that should they not be taken, even if they are not the best choices, one may never get to the desired destination. This was surely the case in our adventure and thus the title of this book. Was there another way to discover a healthy, spiritual, and contributing life? Probably so. But this was our journey and if God is Love, then He needed to work with us where we were at, in the challenges we were facing. So He led us step by step with what we could handle and relate to.

And for those of you who think that the Divine doesn't exist at all, I am not here to try to convince you otherwise. That would be arrogant, and not a part of my experience. But this I can tell you: there were more than a few of us that were involved in this operation at some level, and none of us except one Muslim man were particularly believers of any kind at the start. But throughout the escapade, we felt compelled to admit that Something or Someone was on our side, protecting us, leading us, involved with us. It led us to believe that something other than what we experience on the surface exists. And even more, life takes on more meaning when we discover the deeper layers. So yes, if the core, the essence of the Divine is love, who does not use force to win our love, then He would even join us in our escapade in order to capture our attention and begin to reveal who He is, a God that is on our side. I believe His ultimate goal for us is to understand in our hearts and minds His unconditional love, which is the foundation for healthy, happy relationships now and in the future. That is worth the risk to the Divine, to reach out to us in our journeys, in my case, the journey that included smuggling hash to turn on the world and find meaning and purpose in life. And I believe the Divine stood by us and protected us as we embarked on the next stage of this insane venture.

CHAPTER 20

ROGER

*"I am looking for someone to share in
an adventure that I am arranging, and
it's very difficult to find anyone.
'I should think so—in these parts! We are plain quiet
folk and have no use for adventures. Nasty disturbing
uncomfortable things! Make you late for dinner!'"*

—J. R. R. Tolkien, The Hobbit

Just to be clear, none of us were organized enough to write down the list above and figure out things ahead of time. We just sort of dealt with things as they came along. There was no timetable and no particular goals set. When it was time to get something done, then we worked at it. The project had been sitting in neutral for some time, with no real pressure to move forward. We were content to enjoy the beach. And then we met Roger.

Roger had driven his car from England to Taghazout and was living on the beach in a tent. We got to know him the same way we got to know almost everyone camping on the beach, by sharing a joint or a pipe down at Mohammed's beach café, or virtually anywhere anyone was sitting around, daytime or evening. Big John was a magnet in itself, by being the largest and most visible vehicle on the beach. So after sharing a few pipes with Roger, he became a regular around the bus, listening to stories and music, sharing his own experiences, and enjoying some of Daisy's cooking. You could get to know someone pretty well hanging out on the bus day after day. One night we got to talking about possibilities and "what ifs."

"What if there was a way to conceal a lot of hash in a vehicle and ship it to the USA?" proposed Sky.

"And what if we could find just the right person to drive the vehicle that we could completely trust?" I added.

"I could do something like that," interjected Roger.

No *what if,* he just threw it out there and it kind of shocked us. As we got to know him better, we began to talk to him about our actual plan and our history. Roger was ready to be counted in. We'd found one of the most important pieces of the puzzle and it launched us into full gear.

It was much more than just finding someone to drive the vehicle, a difficult enough task in itself due to issues of trust, ability, etc. Roger was more than just a puzzle piece. He was a perfect fit, beyond our wildest imagination. He looked like an innocent tourist, which is what he was (almost). He was more than sixty years old, fully British (a citizen of the UK), and retired. He had short white hair and a white goatee that looked very distinguished, in a casual way, and could pass for nearly seventy, though he didn't feel old to us. With the twinkle in his round face, he could easily remind you of Saint Nick himself, though he wasn't overweight. He was young at heart, very relaxed in his demeanor, with a glimmer in his eye and a dry British sense of humor. He was likable in every way, and he was single and alone. He had a composed tolerance for risk and was philosophically a hippie. He was a pleasure to have around and became a good friend to all of us. And he was on board in every way. He was helpful in many areas and became a key component in brainstorming ideas.

With Roger now our driver, we planned a trip to England in order to buy the car and camper and look for the chemicals to make the polystyrene panels. Off we went, Sky, Daisy, and me, with Roger leading the way, as he had friends and a lifelong knowledge of the UK.

We shopped for the chemicals first and located them like they were waiting for us…no problem. We figured we needed approximately twenty gallons, so we bought thirty to be safe, fifteen gallons of each chemical, a total of six five-gallon canisters. And we got technical support at the same time. The company who sold us the chemicals understood what we were wanting to do (without the hash part of course) and explained in detail how to accomplish our task. They sold us the additional tools that we needed, or told us where we could get them. One essential tool was a small electric mixer that was basically a three-foot steel shaft with little paddles on the end. It would blend the chemicals together efficiently and could be powered by a gas generator, which we also bought.

Then we shopped for the camper and settled on a nice little used beige model that was just the right size for one person, with a small kitchen, sitting area, double bed, and tiny bathroom. Next we looked for a nondescript two-door sedan, with enough power to pull the camper, considering we would add more than four hundred and fifty pounds (two hundred kilos) to its weight. We got a good deal on a 1967 Ford Cortina, made in England. We figured a Ford would be easy to find parts for if anything went wrong driving across Canada and down to San Francisco. And guess what? The car already had a towing ball installed that was the same size as that which was on the camper.

It could hardly be called a "miracle" finding all the things we needed, but it was certainly a seamless experience that couldn't have gone any more smoothly. It felt like we were on the right track and that we were being "led."

We loaded the five-gallon cylinders into the camper and hooked it up to the Cortina. When Roger got behind the steering wheel to start the journey down to the port, he looked like the epitome of an elder British tourist on extended holiday. There was a ship that sailed out of one of the southern ports of England right into Tangiers harbor. Roger, his car, and his camper would be on it for an especially exciting tour of Morocco. Then he would return to England by the same ship and drive to the port of Southhampton, England. From there he would take an ocean vessel for the next phase of his "holiday" to Canada and ultimately to the USA. The first big chunk of our plan was accomplished and we were ready for the next step, securing the hash. It ended up being a lot more complicated than we originally imagined.

CHAPTER 21

A PRECARIOUS TRIP
IN BIG JOHN

If you come to a fork in the road, take it.

—*Yogi Berra*

It was springtime, 1971, and the next step was to move Big John from the beach at Taghazout, north to wherever we would ultimately find a place to pack the hash. We had never driven Big John any distance at all, but from the short excursions that we had taken, we knew that the bus overheated fairly easily. Our solution was to drive at night, or in the day if it was raining, which was not common. So we began to prepare for our trip north.

All this time Sky, Daisy, and I were attempting to live as two friends with the same woman. Crazy as it may seem, we thought we could make it work. Besides, there was no obvious solution, and we were the free love generation. Daisy was unable to make a decision, and Sky and I had been best friends for a long time. Crosby, Stills & Nash had a song that included the lyrics, "Why can't we go on as three?" We had no life experience or moral compass that said it was impossible and thus we continued the emotionally devastating relationship. It seemed to me that I was the most affected, but we never talked about it. So it's possible we were all suffering severely, except for the wonderful moments that were sprinkled in on a regular basis, enough to keep the dream alive. Besides, we were in the middle of a big deal.

Somewhere around the beginning of April, we began our journey north. We left on a rainy day, but Big John still began to heat up. The goal was to look for puddles on the highway and drive through them. Every time we did, the temperature gauge would drop and Big John was good for another twenty miles. We made it to nightfall and decided to keep going because it was cooler and it was still drizzling.

I was driving and I can still remember this scene like it was yesterday. On Moroccan highways there are occasionally little bridges across a creek or small river. These bridges are not always big enough for two normally sized vehicles at the same time, let alone one the size of Big John. There weren't a lot of cars and trucks on the highways, so it wasn't hard to slow down or speed up, if necessary, to cross the short bridges without stopping.

It was nighttime and Daisy, Sky, and another friend of ours, Daniel, were up at the front of the bus talking with me as I was driving. The visibility was not good due to the darkness, the rain, and Big John's less than award-winning headlights. All of a sudden I realized I was just a hundred feet away from one of those bridges. It was too close to stop and the shoulder on both sides descended sharply down in to the stream or gully the bridge was crossing. We could all see the severe dilemma. I decided in a split second to try to make it across the bridge. The problem was that there was a truck coming from the other direction and it didn't look like there was enough time and space to get off the bridge before colliding. The truck driver had the same options on his side, really no option at all. The four of us went silent. I was now in the middle of the bridge and the truck was approaching the bridge and our previous evaluation was right. There was NOT enough time and space to get off and the truck seemed to be making no effort to slow down or make any adjustment. Visibility was poor for him, too. Even if he was slowing down, we couldn't really tell for certain. What we could tell clearly was that we were in trouble and there was no solution. I don't know if any of the others closed their eyes waiting for the crash, but I didn't. I just swerved to the right as I approached the end of the bridge with such force that it should have flipped Big John and still been hit by the oncoming truck.

Nothing happened. No impact, no flipping, no accident, nothing. I immediately pulled over on the side of the road and just sat there stunned. Daisy, Sky, and Daniel were equally stunned. Nobody said anything for what seemed like a long time, maybe a minute or two. None of us had any idea how we had been spared. Finally, Sky spoke up.

"How did that happen, or how did that not happen?"

"I have no idea. I just waited for the crash."

Nobody had a reasonable explanation. We weren't stoned, we hadn't misjudged the distances; we should have crashed or flipped or both. And we were safe. It was just as pronounced as the miracle in Mexico when my VW bus steered itself back up on to the highway, but this time there were four witnesses.

Four of us all saw the same thing and none of knew how we were spared. Divine intervention of some type was the only explanation that made any sense. We could imagine no other. We had just been part of something that none of us would ever forget and the presence of some kind of Divine escort or partner was sealed in all our minds. Some of us had spoken of it in the past, and it was maybe a good story, or maybe it was real. That night it was real to all of us. We drove just a little farther and found a place to pull over. Even though the weather and temperature was perfect for Big John's radiator problem, the experience was too emotional, too supernatural to be able to just go on. We stopped and talked about it over a few pipes, sitting in Big John late into the night. The journey was on hold for the moment.

The next day was not as eventful, to say the least, but we had to stop many times to let Big John cool off for lack of rain or puddles. We made our way to Tangiers in a few more days and began looking for a place to settle. We met an American who had been living in Morocco longer than any of us, some four years or more. He had become a Muslim and was well connected in many ways. I honestly can't recall the Muslim name he had taken, but it was not a common one like Mohammed. I'll call him Hassan. He lived in Tangiers and also came down to Taghazout. He also knew Roger and would occasionally hang out at the bus. He became aware of our project and said he could help. Personally I didn't connect with Hassan, but thought he could be helpful especially in some of our needs around Tangiers. He did find us a house out in the country about forty-five minutes southeast of Tangiers. It wasn't perfect for what we needed, but it was acceptable. There were just a few houses that were visible to our house, but there were none that were close. The closest was perhaps two to three hundred yards away. It was a somewhat typical Moroccan cement house with an open air flat roof, which would be a good location for our lookouts.

The biggest problem with the house was that it had no garage, barn, or outbuilding where we could hide the camper to disassemble it and then pack it. Barns and outbuildings weren't common enough that we could hope to find one, so we decided to stay there and build one. To make it less obvious, we built it out of straw mats and extended it off of Big John so it looked like we just had a giant enclosed extension off one of the long sides of Big John, an extra outdoor living area that we enclosed on all sides. We built it in a day, and it didn't appear too weird, though I am sure the few Moroccans that saw it probably wondered what it was.

We pulled the camper inside our mat "garage" and began to disassemble it so we could accurately know how much room we had in the walls to place our hash-filled Styrofoam insulation. As soon as we had those dimensions, Sky worked with Daniel to design our mold. Daniel wasn't an engineer, but his design ended up very suitable. Sky constructed two molds side by side, hinged in the middle so it would swing closed. It was the exact thickness of the wall space, about three inches. Fortunately, the wall space was perfect for the normal thickness of Moroccan hash, which is about five-eighths of an inch, and the amount of Styrofoam needed to cover the hash on both sides. We made the mold large enough to accommodate six pieces of hash, each weighing about a pound. The dimensions of each mold was twenty-two inches by twenty-two inches. Each piece of hash was about nine inches by six inches, which would leave about two inches around the edges on all sides for the foam to fill in.

We were ready for our first experiment with the six pieces of hash. We poured the chemicals together in a bucket, fired up the generator, hooked up the electric mixer, and blended the chemical liquids together just like we had been taught. Now it was time to set the hash, each enclosed in a plastic bag, into the mold in a three by two configuration. Then we poured in the chemicals. It was an exciting moment as we clamped our mold shut with wood clamps like we used in shop class when we glued something for an overnight set. Shop class was never so exciting and we remembered for a moment our shop teacher back in high school. If only he had given us some ideas on how we might use what we were learning for something practical like building a mold to pack hash into the walls of a camper. We might have paid better attention.

We waited about fifteen minutes to allow the chemicals to interact and create a hard Styrofoam-type material. We opened the mold for a look at our first product. We looked at each other satisfied. The foam had filled in all around and over the hash. But the other side was still exposed, so we placed it in the second mold, with the exposed side up and repeated the mixing, the pouring, and the sealing of the second mold shut.

The next fifteen-minute-wait took forever, it seemed. As we opened the second mold our confidence was high. The foam had completely surrounded the hash and looked like one solid piece of foam. It was perfect. We placed it in the walls of the camper and it looked like it was factory installed. We laughed, thinking we had improved the energy efficiency of the camper, now better insulated for its upcoming journey. We wondered what the "R- value" of hashish was. Too bad we couldn't

"Google it." Someone likely knew. Anyway, six pounds were ready to go, a little less than three kilos.

We measured the camper walls again to check the square footage. I reran my numbers and was confident that we had enough space for three hundred fifty pounds, maybe a little more. It would require about one hundred ninety five square feet of our foam insulation. When I subtracted out the windows, doors and vents, we had about two hundred square feet of space in the walls for insulation. We didn't dare mess with the ceiling, as the extra weight bouncing along five thousand miles of highway could easily collapse the roof. And none of us were engineers to know for sure. We just figured it wouldn't be safe. And three hundred fifty pounds was a lot of hash. If we could complete one mold procedure from start to finish in about forty-five minutes, we could work about twelve hours a day, pack the camper in four days, and put it back together in one more. Five days would not be long enough for anyone to get overly suspicious about what was happening inside our mat "garage." Until then, our little factory would sit idle while we carried out the next step, perhaps the most dangerous of all. Per usual, we didn't seem to sense that. It was time to get with Absalom and secure the hash.

CHAPTER 22

SECURING THE HASH

In skating over thin ice our safety is in our speed.

—Ralph Waldo Emerson

Two of the things we didn't like about Moroccan hash were that it was a little crumbly and it was light in color. Light in color was a plus for grass, but a negative for hash. The gold standard for hash was from the east, especially Afghanistan. It was dark and very firm, almost sticky. It seemed to be a better quality in almost every characteristic, and of course it fetched a better price on the market. But we wanted nothing to do with that part of the world as it was far too dangerous. Many stories circulated in the hippie community of people being killed or imprisoned without any consideration for personal rights in places like Afghanistan.

But we did want to match their quality and create a better product. We discussed this with Absalom and presented an idea that we had developed during the many nights sitting around Big John letting our creative juices flow. We had an idea for our own special blend. We didn't know anything about how the Afghanis made their hash, but we had an idea how to improve ours, and Absalom was game. In fact he liked it. I can still see the gleam in his friendly and almost playful eyes when he understood what we wanted to do and how it could be accomplished. We felt like we needed to be on-site during production, since the process was new to everyone.

The Rif Mountains in the northeast of Morocco were where most of the kief was grown and the hash was made. It was unusual for non-Arabs to come into the area where the kief was grown and even more so where the hash was made, but we knew there would be some tweaking along the way and we wanted to be there. We gave Absalom a couple of days to make arrangements, and we were off to the mountains of Morocco.

We left at night in a van with someone Absalom had arranged to meet us. He drove us within a few miles of our destination. Then we walked at night with lanterns about three to four miles up into the hills. The nice thing about djellabas is you really can't tell anything about anyone if you have the hood up. And at night almost everyone has their hood up, so we arrived without any suspicion. It seemed like a country farmhouse; it was quite large but had a comfortable feeling to it, with the typical mats on the floor and low sofa beds around a table. Absalom had graciously arranged a delicious supper of vegetable tagine for us. Daisy especially relished the homemade round Moroccan bread that we all dipped into the tagine on the table in the middle. We smoked a few pipes together, talked very little, but smiled a lot. We slept soundly on straw mats on the floor, feeling satisfied on every level.

When morning came they had already begun experimenting with our new recipe. The plan was simple, as most decent ideas usually are. Hash in Morocco is made by first harvesting the kief when it is very dry and removing the buds and flowers from the stalk of the female plant. Then, by agitating or beating the buds and flowers, the pollen is separated and sifted out. The extracted pollen is then placed inside a plastic bag to be pressed in a simple hydraulic press. There are enough natural oils in the pollen that it holds together after it comes out of the press, but in the case of Moroccan hash, not very well. As I mentioned before, it is a little crumbly, and occasionally it can revert nearly to a pollen form, like tiny crumbs. Our idea was to cook the kief mixed with water in a large vat and simmer it until it became thick. As the water evaporated, we would lightly push the kief leaves against a screen to try to press some more of the resin or oils out. Little by little the remaining liquid would get darker and thicker and stickier.

Cooks will do this with balsamic vinegar sometimes to make what is called balsamic reduction and use it as part of a salad dressing. It removes the vinegar bite and enhances the balsamic flavor. We weren't going for a flavor change, but a texture and color change. When the liquid was deemed thick and sticky enough by us, it was mixed with the pollen and pressed. We could see that the color was better, but would it be a good binder and make the hash less crumbly? We waited for the first block to come out of the press. Sky and I broke off a small piece and crumbled it in our fingers while Absalom and Daisy looked on. It was much firmer, much stickier. We couldn't say it was Afghan quality, but we felt it was the best Moroccan hash that had ever been made. And it was our own formula.

Now it needed a name to compete with Afghan Black or Lebanese Gold, etc. We smoked a pipe or two together and a name came into my head. I didn't know it yet, but as it turns out, I had a head for marketing, which I describe simply as the ability to sense what other people will feel about your product by the way you present it. For those of you who were *Mad Men* enthusiasts, you know how hard Madison Avenue works to come up with a few words to describe a product that will stick in people's heads. "See the USA in your Chevrolet," "Fly the friendly skies of United," and sometimes it's just one word or phrase: "the Pepsi Generation." In this case, it was just one word, and everybody liked it instantly:

"BLOTTO," I said enthusiastically. *"It doesn't mention the word 'Morocco,' which is not a positive for hash, but it does refer to exceptional results."*

"Blotto." It sounded like a winner. For the moment, we forgot about all the risks and enjoyed the "Now." "Be Here Now." It may not have been exactly what Baba Ram Das had in mind, but it sort of fit. We were definitely in the moment. But the moment would pass quickly when the police arrived.

CHAPTER 23

PACKING THE CARAVAN AND THE ARRIVAL OF THE POLICE

A journey is like a marriage. The certain way
to be wrong is to think you control it.

—John Steinbeck

"The moment" held fast through what we expected to be the most dangerous steps of the mission. But in fact, getting the hash made and transported out to our country home and makeshift garage went surprisingly smoothly. Having all of that hash concentrated in one place was definitely nerve-racking. We tried to hide it under our bed in the back of Big John, knowing that would not be sufficient in any raid; it made us feel a little better, but not really. The next chore was to organize our team for the ambitious job of hiding close to four hundred pounds of hash in the walls of our little vacation home on wheels. Daisy, Sky, and I stayed in Big John, while the rest of our crew stayed in the house with their mats on the floor and sleeping bags.

While the simple square white stucco house had no running water or electricity, compared to some other houses in the area it was a virtual "villa." Like many similar Moroccan houses, it had a flat roof enclosed by a four-foot-high concrete wall, and a staircase leading up to it on the inside of the house. It could be used to do laundry, sunbathe, or sleep under the stars in relative privacy and security. It also offered a view for several miles in every direction with clear sight along the only road in the area, which passed by about thirty feet in front of the house. We posted two full-time watchmen up on the roof. They were to keep us informed about any activity along that road whenever we were working. At least that was the plan.

We began the process of making our molds to contain the hash. Inside Big John, Daniel maintained a clay pot charcoal cook stove and kept several long chef's knives hot over the coals. He was surrounded by stacks of hash plates. I would call my orders in through the window of the bus and Daniel would cut pieces to size from the plates and pass them out to me. I would then put them in plastic bags and arrange them in the first bay of the press to match the spaces in the camper walls with a small margin around each edge.

Once the pieces were arranged, I would call out "PRESS!" Sky would come in from the camper, Daniel would run in from the bus, and the drill was on. It took all three of us to mix the foam, pour it, then close and secure the press with several lengths of 4"x4" lumber and some large carpenter's clamps. It was a little disorganized at first, but we soon became a well-oiled machine. Daniel got a bit wobbly at times because every piece of hash he cut with the hot knives sent a plume of smoke directly into his nostrils. He called it his "dream job."

After the foam set up, the press was opened, the sheet of foam and hash was turned over into the second bay, and the first bay was ready for a new arrangement. So after the first press, foam was poured into both bays and each repetition yielded one half-completed and one fully completed piece of foam with no hash visible. Those would then be cut to the predetermined shape and trimmed with a foam shaving tool that Sky had been thoughtful enough to remember. He seemed to enjoy shaving the pieces, so they fit snug into the walls of the camper. It looked like factory-installed insulation and an artistic jigsaw puzzle.

At first we worked mostly at night because, "the cops don't come out at night in Morocco." We worried that the neighbors (mostly shepherds) might get disturbed about the *zing, zing, zinnnnngggggg* of the foam mixing drill that must have carried for miles across that silent plateau. And each morning, a minute or so of flames and a huge puff of black smoke rising from a fifty-five gallon oil drum where we disposed of accumulated scraps of foam and signaled to the world the end of another night of our hard labor.

By day, the hash was hidden back under the bed where there was also a trap door in the floor of Big John. The camper was roughly restored to an inconspicuous condition. Daisy kept us well fed while we got whatever sleep we could during the day. The problem was it was simply taking too long. Too much time was spent trying to cover our tracks. We decided to work during the day and rely on the lookouts to watch our backs. We didn't have any real plan for what we would do if the police came. I guess we just didn't want to think about that happening and therefore we blotted it out and kept on going. It left us with no escape plan, nothing.

It was late one dreary afternoon. We had been making good progress, but hash and camper parts were strewn around almost recklessly as a result of our furious pace. I don't know whether the lookouts were sitting on the roof rolling another joint or if they were passed out on the floor, or what. The one thing they were certainly not doing was looking down the several miles of visible road leading up to our house to see if any vehicles were approaching.

Even three minutes would have provided time to make an honest effort to hide the evidence. But the next thing any of us working in our "factory" knew was that a police car had pulled up and stopped on the road right in front of our house. Who actually saw it or who called out the alarm I am not sure. It was a knee jerk reaction for me. Using the house as a shield I took off walking briskly through the field that was next to our house and tried to disappear into the neighborhood. But as I mentioned earlier, there wasn't much of a neighborhood. The nearest house was at least a few hundred yards away, and the next house another few hundred yards beyond that, so it wasn't like I had much opportunity to disappear into anything. Nevertheless, I just took off in broad daylight with my djellaba hood up and kept walking, with my heart beating hard. The first thing I took notice of was that I had walked a few minutes and no one was yelling at me, no guns were being fired, and I heard nothing. So I just kept walking, through fields and past a house or two.

Finally, I got far enough away to where I stopped behind a tree and ventured a peek out from under my hood back in the direction of our house. I could see the house and Big John and our garage in the distance, but I couldn't make out any activity. I used the tree as my vantage point for a while. I didn't really think about what might be happening back there, I was focused on trying to figure out if anything was happening at all. There seemed to be no ruckus of any kind. It was very still, like a quiet, lazy Saturday afternoon. I'm not quite sure how long I stayed away, but finally I saw one of our group walking around near the house and I decided to cautiously return to the scene. The closer I got the more it seemed like nothing was happening so I walked to get into a position where I could see the road again and be able to discern whether the police car was still there.

The typical Moroccan police car was a small boxy European black sedan. They rarely had a bubble gum machine on top, or any obvious markings, like our typical black and white. They normally did have official markings on the side that said police or something similar, but it was rather understated. Since Morocco was French, historically, and they use the word "police," that is generally what was written on their cars to identify them. In any case, when I got in position to see the road in front of our house, there was no vehicle there of any kind. I walked back to the house and Sky saw me coming and met me just outside Big John.

"What happened?" I asked incredulously.

"They just came and sat there for a while in the car and split," answered Sky, with a look of dismay, fear, and exhilaration all mixed together.

"Wow!" There was really not much more one could say.

For the next thirty minutes or so, we all sat around and listened to what anyone knew about what happened. One of our lookouts recounted his experience. He was up on the roof, sitting down, smoking a joint, when he thought he heard something. Lots of times when you're stoned you think you hear something and it's nothing, but he stood up to look over the wall of the roof. And there it was, a cop car had just pulled up and stopped in front of our property, the nose of their car about even with the front edge of the house. He didn't wait to see if they got out of the car, he just ran downstairs and told anyone in his path that the police had just pulled up outside.

What had everyone done? Sky didn't want to raise any additional suspicion so he stayed and joined Daisy, who remained on Big John. Others stayed in the house, just waiting. Daniel went up on the roof to take a fresh look over the wall. It was maybe five or ten minutes after the police arrived that he took "the look." They were just sitting there in the car. Were they waiting for backup, or what? Daniel slipped back down to the bus and helped Sky and Daisy in a chaotic and futile effort to hide the hash, etc. Then about ten minutes later he thought he heard movement outside. He went back up and took another look. The police car was turning around and leaving! He watched as it drove into the distance.

"You mean they just sat there and never got out of the car?"

Sky and Daisy recounted how they had wondered for a moment where I was going and what my plan was if any, but quickly forgot about me and did their best to clean up whatever was lying around and obvious. The camper was partially disassembled, of course, and what was going on would have been very obvious to anyone who was there to bust us, but still it felt best to do what they could. So they kept busy the whole time until Daniel reported their departure.

"You mean they just sat there and then turned around and left?" I repeated.

We were all still incredulous. Had the Divine hand held the police at bay and said, *this far and no farther*? Why in the world had the police driven all the way out into the country, down the long country road, parked right outside our house, and just sat there and did nothing? The sense of something unusual, something mystical, continued to grow among us. No one had a good explanation and so we took the one that felt the best and perhaps the most reasonable if you could take the leap into believing in Someone. Could the Divine of this world actually have an interest in us...in me? Frodo's question resurfaced in my mind, "What kind of story have we fallen into?" Is God a part of the story, and does He care? Is He truly involved in the lives of men and women, His children in this world? If so, why sometimes and not other times? Or is it we who are just too distracted most of the time to be aware?

I am not saying we were interpreting all that was happening accurately, or that we even all agreed, but in some way we all felt special at some indescribable level. None of us would have insisted that all of what we were experiencing was nothing but good luck. Maybe Einstein was right, "Coincidence is God's way of remaining anonymous." Like the question posed in the movie *The Life of Pi*: "Which story do you prefer?" I preferred the idea of Divine involvement and most, if not all, agreed. It seemed to make the most sense and it was definitely the most romantic.

Looking back, I wonder if there was really any other way the Divine could make contact with us. If recognizing the Spirit in our lives depended upon us first getting in a good place, then how would anyone ever get there? I now conclude that the Divine meets us where we are, in our nonsense, in our pride, in our depression, in our fears, in our adventure. Wherever we are, if a moment arises where we will listen, He is there. Like a lover, planning an encounter to "bump into" the one he or she is seeking, the Divine Lover waits: not passively, but in a more intricate, ingenious way than we might imagine. The Spirit awakens us to a reality outside ourselves that catches our attention. And if we follow on, we find the Tracker is on our side, and the best thing that could ever happen to us.

We laid low for the rest of the day and night, wondering if they would possibly come back, but with no activity by the next morning, we were busily back to work with new intensity to get the job done and safely conceal the hash in the walls of the camper. Our lookouts were inspired to be more vigilant, and the rest of us were doing our jobs as before. Our rhythm was better than ever, and one by one the press spit out sheets of Styrofoam insulation. Two more days measuring, cutting, molding, dissembling, and reassembling and the camper was done. When we were finished, every last piece had passed through the press and into the walls. We barely had enough hash to smoke. We debated for a moment that we were starving ourselves of ample personal supplies. But, every pound we packed into the camper was about eight hundred dollars more back home and we had estimated perfectly. The bottom line though, we really didn't want to have any quantity around anymore. It felt good to be almost clean.

All we had left to do was some touch up work and we wanted to move out of where we were. The visit from the police still haunted us, so we decided to drive the camper to some place that was like a state park about an hour away and do the finishing touches there. Driving down the road, pulling the camper behind us, was a weird feeling. It felt dangerous, but exhilarating, mingled with a sense of pride and satisfaction all at the same time. We pulled into the state park at dusk and camped there for the night. The next morning we started our finishing work.

There were just a few things that needed some attention: panels that had been damaged in the dissembling process that needed to be fitted better or repaired a little and/or touched up with paint. We had brought some paint from England for that very reason. There was a bench seat inside against the wall that when you lifted up the seat, our poly mold was visible as there was no panel on the inside. It was while we had that open and were measuring to put a piece of one-eighth inch plywood to cover it, that, believe it or not, the police showed up again.

Daisy was inside the camper and Sky and I were outside working on something. As their vehicle pulled up, we both walked off quickly in different directions into the woods. But the woods surrounding us were thin (typical of a state park) and I knew the police had seen me, so I turned around and came back. I saw Daisy talking with one of the policemen. If anyone was ever good at talking to officials of any kind, it was Daisy. I had seen her do it a dozen times, from traffic police in Mexico, Spain, and Morocco, to customs agents at whatever border we were crossing. She was mesmerizing. First of all she was blond, curvaceous, and beautiful. Second of all, she was friendly and engaging. Third, she could usually speak the language—French, Spanish, or Arabic—and that was always disarming and captivating to the official, or whoever it was. And sure enough, she seemed to be at it again.

But as I approached them, they wanted to know why I had run away. They hadn't seen Sky run so it was just me. They were French-speaking Moroccan policemen and my French was quite fluent from six years of high school and college French and a year living in Grenoble. I explained I wasn't running, I just had to go take a pee really badly and they happened to be pulling up at that very moment. I knew it was a pretty lame excuse, but I rattled away in French, explaining more than I needed to. Fortunately, Daisy had already set the tone by telling them that we were camping there and how much we loved Morocco and the wonderful people with so much enthusiasm and genuine sincerity that somehow they accepted it.

And the best part? They never set foot inside the camper with the bench seat open and a small amount of hash that Daisy stashed in a drawer when they pulled in. And they never looked around or asked some obvious questions about what we were repairing, painting, etc. They pulled away; we didn't know why they came or whether there was something going on connected to the other police encounter. Maybe they were setting us up for the big bust at the right moment. Or perhaps it was another, *this far and no farther*, another case of the Protective Hand over us. Regardless, for the first time, we felt strongly that we wanted to hustle out of Morocco and move into the next phase. Life in a Moroccan jail never really entered our minds or crossed our lips. It probably should have. It might have kept us from such insanity. But it didn't. The day finished uneventfully and we didn't even talk about what had just happened. Our eyes and body language told the whole story. It was time to pass off the vehicle to Roger and begin the trip to England.

CHAPTER 24

ACROSS THE OCEAN AND UPSTATE BOB

The reason people find it so hard to be happy
is that they always see the past better than
it was, the present worse than it is, and the
future less resolved than it will be.

—Marcel Pagnol

Sky volunteered to accompany Roger to England. It was the most practical decision since he was the most mechanical if anything went wrong. And someone had to stay with the stuff. We learned that lesson well from the Gerty experience, even though Roger was no Gerty. The camper would never leave our sight again, or almost never. Roger booked a passage on the ship from Tangiers to England and he and Sky boarded the ship, though separately so as not to arouse suspicion or indicate that they were friends. Daisy and I took the ferry to Algeciras, Spain, and from there drove to Lisbon in my VW bus.

We were clean; squeaky clean. Unlike Morocco, it was dangerous to get caught in Spain or Portugal with the smallest trace of hash or any other drug for that matter. The Guardia Civil were a fearful presence and had a reputation for being very tough military police. We made sure our bodies, our clothing, and our vehicle were completely hash and kief free. We checked all the drawers and pockets, every nook and corner that we could find or imagine. We went through all our clothing to make sure we hadn't left something in a shirt or pants pocket (it seemed like all my shirt and pants pockets contained a little piece of hash). We also knew we would eventually be entering the USA in New York and my beard and thick head of hair that hung down to my waist were sure to arouse suspicion. Strip searches were not uncommon. Daisy's charm would not be worth much with US Customs or the Guardia Civil. We had to be clean, and that was all there was to it.

Arriving in Lisbon, we boarded the infamous *Yugolinea*, the same freighter in which she and Sky had gone through the hurricane. For some reason, it didn't seem to faze her to climb onto that ship again. Maybe it was that so much danger and so many close calls had already happened, maybe because she was with me and that changed the atmosphere, or maybe it was just being young. But she and I took the freighter together to New York. It was the end of June, 1971, and we sailed out into the Atlantic for what we both hoped would be an uneventful crossing.

Meanwhile, unbeknownst to Daisy and me, the decision to send Sky with Roger and the camper proved to be very wise, since it prevented a disaster. During their voyage to England, a car next to Roger's camper came loose and struck it and damaged it sufficiently to expose some of the hash! Sky had to repair it before the ship got to England, which somehow he was able to accomplish. Roger and the camper cruised through customs and he and Sky made their way down to Southampton for Roger's voyage to Montreal. When the ship sailed with Roger and the camper safely on it, Sky made his way back to London and a flight home to New York City.

While all that was happening, Daisy and I were crossing the Atlantic, and we were alone! There were about ten or fifteen other passengers and roughly the same number of crew, but for a week it wasn't the three of us, something we hadn't experienced even for a full twenty-four hours since becoming lovers. She and Sky had a few times like that, when I was chasing Jenny or some other distraction, but this was our first and it was sort of like a honeymoon. For a few days, I forgot that it would end and it felt like we were meant to be together. It seemed she loved me and I was sure I loved her and we loved being together, just the two of us. There was zero entertainment on the ship, as this was a freighter. We were served meals with the crew and the other passengers in a very basic dining room, like a school cafeteria only built for forty people. That was the only planned activity three times a day. Young and in love, we managed to enjoy the free time.

Reality began to set in as we neared New York, however. This little pleasure cruise was about to end and it would be back to three and worse than that, there would be the abandonment. As I mentioned earlier, the only way Daisy could deal with this impossible relationship was to set me aside when it was time to give attention to Sky. I felt that to an extreme, which I guess would be normal, but there was no "normal" in this mess. And now we had just had a honeymoon together and I knew what was coming. It didn't seem fair to be utterly set aside, right after the honeymoon, for another guy. I didn't blame Sky. How could I? He was caught in the middle the way I was and I was the newcomer, the intruder so to speak. And I didn't blame Daisy, either; she was in an unworkable situation, too. But couldn't she find some better way to deal with it all? Apparently not. The pain came quickly. We breezed through customs with a thorough but not excessive search.

Sky met us at the dock and it was "good-bye to me" time. Yes, we were all three together, but it was like I didn't exist to Daisy. As we drove up to Montreal, I had to just be a fly on the wall while I watched her pour love and affection on Sky; and there was no escape. The honeymoon was lost and the pain set in. My whole mind and body and soul were suffering. I didn't know if I could make it. And when Daisy saw my pain, and that I couldn't handle it well, she estranged herself from me all the more. Somehow she expected me to just deal with it. She was probably right, but I had no idea how to do that.

Sky talked about how things went on the trip to England, the damage from the vehicle breaking loose and about seeing Roger and the camper off on the ship to Montreal. I wasn't listening. I was lost in so many mixed emotions it was enough to drive a person crazy. Can misery and frustration and love and anxiety and pain and depression somehow all exist at the same time? Not for very long. Something had to give and it was going to be me, though there was so much left to the story of which I was unaware. For starters, the drive to Montreal was about to take our minds off of our problem by giving us something else to think about.

It is a three hundred and fifty-mile drive from New York City due north to Montreal, right up the long straight eastern edge of New York State. About halfway there, a New York State cop pulled alongside my VW bus. Sky was driving at the time, and the three of us were classic hippies in looks and attire, all sitting together on the bench seat in the front of the van. Some parts of upstate New York seemed quite redneck in attitude at the time, and once this cop saw who was in the front seat, he began drooling at the thought of a hippie drug bust. He pulled us over and after the license and registration drill, he began to interrogate us.

"Where are you going? Why are you driving up to Canada?"

"Because here in the States, cops like you stop us for no reason," I retorted, leaning in from the passenger side.

This was a case of two enemies meeting face-to-face and we glared at each other with disdain. Soon, we were out of the bus and he was searching the van for dope. There was no search warrant, no thought of illegal search and seizure. Certain that we had the contraband, this state "bear" was determined to find it. He was sure he would bust us. What he didn't know was that we were just off the boat and we knew we were clean. I felt fearless and empowered. Indignant about the violation of our rights, I began egging him on. As he pulled out our suitcases and began to search them, I gave him suggestions about where to look. I had gotten my Ph.D. at Andover in sarcasm and cynicism and my current disturbed state of mind gave me permission to pour it on.

"Didn't they give you any training in police academy to know where to search? Did you check all the pockets in the clothing?"

And then when he began to look in our clothing and the pockets:

"Do you really think we would hide our stash in our pockets? Wouldn't we want it more accessible than that? Think man, think. There must be some secret compartment somewhere. How about down in the gas tank? Have you got a rubber tube in your cop car to siphon out the gas? Why are you even looking in the glove compartment? Do you really think we are going to hide our grass in the glove compartment? Did you look under the mats? What about under the bed? Everybody keeps their valuables under their mattress. Here, let me help you, the mattress is a little heavy. By the way, what do you keep under your mattress? Does your wife know about it?"
I said that with a little wink, man to man.

Officer Robert (I caught his name tag) was not enjoying my banter that went on for a good forty-five minutes to an hour. My verbal diarrhea, insults, and degrading sarcasm did not stop until every last item was out of the van and onto the side of the road; every bag, backpack, pocketbook, drawer… everything. It was quite a spectacle. Every car that drove by was slowing down to take a look. We were waving and smiling and inviting them to pull over and join the fun. They all drove right by. I was now on a first name basis with Robert, and Sky and Daisy were joining in with an occasional comment.

"Bob," I said, *"do you mind if I call you Bob?"*

"My name is Robert," he replied gruffly.

"Bob," I said ignoring him, *"Bob, maybe you could call for backup, find someone with more experience in searching hippies. Come on Bob, think. You haven't searched our bodies yet. Have you thought about that… Bob?"*

Maybe he was worried about cars driving by and seeing three hippies running around naked, but he never searched our bodies, except our pockets. His frustration and irritation was maxing out.

"C'mon Bob, don't give up now. You've got to persevere, press forward, onward and upward...Bob. How are you ever going to advance in rank if you can't even bust a few hippies. Oh, but by the way Bob, we don't smoke that stuff. It makes us cough and our moms told us that it's not good for us and we love our moms Bob. Do you love your mom...Bob?"

Finally...Bob gave up. With not much ado, he just climbed into his patrol car as if he'd gotten an important call and drove off leaving our mess behind. We put things back together, loaded them back into the bus, and headed on our way again. I sat in the back seat as we started off again, a bit exhausted from my own excessive, irreverent banter and our afternoon in the sun. We were all a little thirsty so I got out some water to drink. I found a few Dixie cups in a cup holder on the side door next to where I was sitting. I separated the cups to pour each of us a drink. My eyes popped and my mouth dropped. Daisy was looking back at me waiting for me to hand her the cups. Then she saw the horror in my eyes.

"What is it?" she asked.

"You won't believe what's between the Dixie cups."

I paused for effect. And then I pulled out a chunk of hash big enough to fill the bottom of the cup, hidden by the cup that was stuck on top of it. It had made it all the way from Morocco into Spain, across Portugal and into the USA, undetected by our best cleaning efforts and the border controls of each country. And now undetected even by Upstate Bob! The three of us imagined for a moment what Bob would have done to us (me in particular) if he had found that unknown piece of hash. We laughed and shivered at the same time. Well, somehow, once again for some reason, it didn't happen.

Apparently, the Divine was still on our side, or at least we concluded, He wasn't on the side of the police trying to bust "innocent" hippies! That latest incident of protection kept our little project from being completely derailed. We imagined what would have happened. Roger would have arrived in Montreal and there would have been no one there to meet him and no one who knew what had happened to us or where to find us…in jail. No cell phones, no communication, no plan. Anyway, now we had a different problem, one we knew how to solve. What do we do with this piece of hash? We wouldn't dare cross the Canadian border with it. It would be irreverent to throw it out, or…we looked at each other with a fresh light in our eyes. We drove another few hours, pulled over at a camp ground for the night and smoked it all before we slept a good night's sleep.

CHAPTER 25

WELCOME TO CANADA

Life is always a rich and steady time when you are waiting for something to happen or to hatch.

—E. B. White, Charlotte's Web

It was only fifty more miles before we'd cross into Canada, a friendlier country to hippies, and now a safe haven for young men seeking to avoid the draft. Canada, like many countries, was generally against the war in Vietnam. We all felt better crossing into Canada. We reached Montreal the day before the ship arrived from England and we were at the dock early the next morning when it pulled in. We located a vantage point from which to watch the ship as it docked and though fairly far away we could see people on the various decks of the ship. Our eyes searched for Roger. I was nicknamed Legolas (from Tolkien's *Lord of the Rings*) for my good long distance eyesight, and sure enough I spotted him. "He's up against the railing on the top level below the smokestack. Do you see him?" Neither Sky or Daisy could see him. He was more than a few hundred yards off. It seemed to me like he saw us, but if he did, he looked away.

What should have been the tensest moment so far was upon us, but we were more excited than nervous. How exhaustive would Roger's border inspection be? Would our "artwork" endure the scrutiny? We waited in our van about five blocks from the exit path of vehicles coming off the ship. Our stomachs tightened more with every minute and if we had waited an hour, it would have been excruciating. Fortunately, a vehicle pulling a camper appeared and in it was a smug and victorious Roger, driving calmly down the road and looking to us like a dream come true. We followed him at a distance before briefly connecting with him at a gas station about twenty minutes outside of Montreal. We didn't tarry to visit until we had driven a couple more hours. Then we stopped and had a little picnic together and got the lowdown on his voyage and his border crossing. It was a totally uneventful experience, just a couple of questions regarding the purpose of his visit. In his quaint British accent, he repeated for us his short conversation with the customs agent about his dream trip touring Canada and the USA. It all sounded so perfect.

I rode with Roger now to keep him company and later to give him a rest from driving. It was a welcome break for me to get away from the Sky and Daisy reunion, which despite all the excitement, still had me at a high level of internal exasperation.

"I don't know if I can handle this much longer," I confided. *"It's just eating me up."*

Roger was the only human being that had ever asked me how I survived in the relationship. I still remember his simple answer back in his brief, very English precision:

"I don't know how you manage, man."

"I'm not sure if I am managing," I confessed.

Though the conversation about "that" went no further, I felt relief for the first time in the last few days. Roger was a comfortable and warm type besides being an interesting person. And I didn't have to watch Daisy be all loving toward Sky while abandoning me. And the obvious truth was I wasn't managing. I was barely enduring.

The next day it was time for Sky to ride with Roger for a while. Daisy and I got separated from them while we were getting gas and suddenly a violent thunder, rain, and lightning storm blew up around us. We pulled over because it became hard to see and we did not want to accidentally pass them and risk losing each other completely. Oh, for a cell phone! At least we knew for certain that they were ahead of us. When the storm passed, we headed out again and soon saw them parked just off the highway. Sky always was a good storyteller, but Roger confirmed this one with his eyes and body language as Sky described it for us. They pulled over just as we had, but it was as if the lightning hovered right over them.

"Bolt after bolt struck all around us, one after another with deafening impact. The thunder claps shook the car, the camper, and us, too. The lightning was so close and intense it was almost blinding, making us feel like we were inside the light. We thought we were going down, just waiting for the next bolt to finish us off. For a moment we both looked at each other with the unspoken thought of how bizarre to go down in this manner after all we had been through. After ten minutes of intense fear, it finally passed."

Sky gave Daisy a meaningful look.

"It was like the hurricane all squeezed into ten minutes."

Daisy caught the analogy easily and gave Sky an empathetic hug. They were both still very shaken. In fact, they had been frozen there nearly speechless until we showed up. They took some time to recover and then it was back on the road with a new conversation piece.

The protection went on. We almost expected it.

That night, somewhere in Ontario, we met the local version of the Canadian state bird (summer variety), also known as the mosquito. We pulled over into an official campground. We thought it strange that everyone's lights were out and no one met us at the gate to check us in.

It was less than an hour after dusk, maybe around 9:00 or 9:30 p.m. We pulled into an available site and got out to stabilize the camper for the night. Within seconds the mosquitoes found us. We forced ourselves to complete the job in just a minute or so, while slapping madly at the attackers. We jumped into the camper and closed the door quickly behind us, but a dozen or so made it in with us. We furiously smashed them into oblivion but more were finding their way in. Everywhere we looked another mosquito emerged from cracks and crevices we would swear did not exist. I pulled back the curtains to look outside and saw thousands of mosquitoes surrounding the camper. I screamed.

"It's Alfred Hitchcock's movie, The Birds. *Only it's The Mosquitoes!"*

It was not so much in fear as in sheer awe of the power such tiny and fragile creatures could exert over us when massed together in countless numbers. We were being held hostage by a hoard of gossamer little bugs and it was freaking us out. It was crazy, a seemingly unrealistic reality, but we had no choice but to deal with it.

There was only one solution. We had to throw ourselves back out directly into the invading force, wind up the stabilizers, and flee for our lives. Sky and I dressed to cover every inch of our body, pulling socks over our pants, scarves around our necks, and wool hats over our heads that we found in the luggage. Roger ran to the car and Daisy to the VW bus and started their engines. Sky and I tried to complete our tasks as quickly as possible.

"How are you doing over there man?" I cried out in the dark to Sky.

"Almost done with the last stabilizer," he replied loudly, spitting out mosquitoes as he spoke.

I was suffering the same experience. There were so many of them. We jumped into the vehicles, sped away and drove for hours until we found another area that we tested before bedding down. It seemed we had escaped. We spent the night in relative peace.

A couple of uneventful days on the road ate up many miles and brought us close to our crossing point into the USA. We were on a steady march across Canada, and quite focused. Our goal was in sight. We looked for a touristy location as (after all) Roger was touring Canada and the USA for his once-in-a-lifetime retirement excursion. We chose Metaline Falls, a small border town in Washington State that was quite sleepy but still in the mountains and near a national forest. We thought about crossing at Sweetgrass, a small border crossing in Montana, but thought any name with grass in it just seemed too perfect. Besides, my license still showed my home address of Weed Street. Let's not have some customs agent in Sweetgrass start asking questions about my address of Weed Street. It would have definitely added to the story, but reason prevailed and we went with what seemed a safer bet.

About an hour before we reached Metaline Falls, we left Roger to drive by himself. We followed just behind until we got to Metaline and then we gave him about a five-minute lead. We weren't expecting any drama and we didn't have any. They didn't even bother the three of us in my VW bus. And when we caught up with Roger, he told us of the nice, short chat he had with the border agent after he briefly checked his passport.

"How is your trip going sir?" asked the border agent, a pleasant man in his fifties.

"I have been motoring all over the Queen's Canada and except for some mosquitoes in Ontario, it has been one delightful day after another. I now I am hoping my first trip to your country will be equally pleasant."

"I am sure you will find our country even more inspiring, sir. Welcome to the United States of America!" And he waved him forward.

CHAPTER 26

STEVE AND THE SANTA CRUZ MOUNTAINS

The happiness of one's own heart alone cannot satisfy the soul; one must try to include, as necessary to one's own happiness, the happiness of others.

—Paranahasa Yogananda

We were home free with just the drive to San Francisco ahead of us and the final phase of the journey. We were eager to arrive and we made it the following afternoon. While San Francisco was our general destination, we were actually headed about sixty file miles south of it to Santa Cruz. We stopped to call Charles from a payphone.

"Hey man, where are you?" came Charles voice excitedly over the line.

"We are just an hour away from San Fran," I replied with equal elation.

It was only the second time we had spoken to him since we left Africa, the first being shortly after our safe arrival in Montreal.

"I'll meet you just south of the Golden Gate bridge on Route 1."

We knew exactly where he meant. He met us on the highway and led us down the beautiful Pacific coast for our last scenic drive before delivery. When we arrived in Santa Cruz we headed inland and then up into the nearby mountains. As much as the drop off point for the grass from Mexico had been short on privacy, this one was perfect. We felt like we were in the middle of nowhere, and we were. We wound around on mountain roads, into the forest of beautiful majestic redwoods and then onto a dirt road that led deeper into the forest. Another ten minutes on the dirt road and we turned into a small clearing, a lovely spot to camp with no one nearby, except for Steve.

Steve was renting and caretaking a five hundred-acre property, living in a cabin that was about a ten-minute walk or three-minute drive from where we parked. He met us at the clearing, an upbeat, high energy, engaging hippie about our age. He was excited about who we were and what we had just accomplished, but soon encouraged us to take off and leave the stripping of the vehicle to him and his team. Before we took off, however, we removed that panel we had installed at the very end (at the park where the Moroccan police came) so we could show him and Charles the hash and have everybody check it out. It was definitely a moment of pride for us, to remove the polystyrene panel and break it open to reveal the hash inside. There was almost a little hush until Steve's enthusiasm broke the silence.

"Far out, man. You guys really did a right on job!"

Everybody's eyes were bright as we removed the hash from the plastic bag and they saw the darker than expected color and that it was not as crumbly as typical Moroccan hash. Charles was always quite calm. Steve was especially animated.

"Blotto! What a great name, and what a great looking product! People are going to get off on this!"

He assured us that they would be able to unload it quickly and at better than average prices. Nobody indulged in smoking any of it at that time. It seemed it was time to get down to business. There would be plenty of time to enjoy life together later on. There was trust on all sides and we were happy to leave it in their hands. This was their business. We were not dealers, we were smugglers. Our work was done. Now we would wait. And we didn't have to wait long.

Two days later we were back at Steve's. He and his team had sold it all. We were hoping for eight hundred dollars per pound and he got us eight hundred and fifty. We never asked him what he made, nor did we seek to know what Charles made. But we weren't quite sure what to make of about three hundred thousand dollars in cash! These were the days when a coke was ten cents, a fancy car was five thousand dollars, and gasoline was thirty to forty cents a gallon. We bought two hundred and fifty acres of land the next year on Cape Breton island in Canada for fifty dollars an acre. For argument's sake, by today's standard, it would probably have been the equivalent of over four million dollars, a lot more than that at street value. Whatever it was, it was a lot of money and we were overwhelmed by it, to say the least. We were never into this whole enterprise exclusively for the money and this was more than we had ever thought about. As you have probably discerned by now, there is a lot we didn't really think about. The payoff was almost all in hundreds so it could fit in a fireproof metal box that Steve was thoughtful enough to give to us. We hid our metal box in the trunk of one of the redwood trees about a two-minute walk from our campsite.

For the few days we camped on his property and hung out in the evenings at his cabin smoking blotto and many other specialty brands he kept on hand. It was like blowing off steam, or coming down from some type of a drug-induced "high." We had been living with such intensity since we'd left the beach at Taghazout that it was a knee-jerk reaction to exhale a mighty sigh of relief now that it was over. And it was over, or so it seemed. But like Yogi said, "It ain't over till it's over." He couldn't have been more right in our case. We had no idea what was ahead. It was not what we expected.

CHAPTER 27

BUSTED, NANTUCKET, AND BACK TO MOROCCO

Yesterday, all my troubles seemed so far away
Now it looks as though they're here to stay
Oh I believe in yesterday
Suddenly I'm not half the man I used to be
There's a shadow hanging over me
Oh, yesterday came suddenly

—Paul McCartney

We paid Roger his twenty-five thousand dollars and might have given him an extra five thousand. I can't recall for sure. We parted ways until we would meet again in Morocco a few months later. We didn't have the heart to drive across the country again so I let a friend drive my van for me. He got a free trip east for his effort along with a generous stash of hash for the journey. We saved a few kilos for personal use that we hid in the walls behind the mats. We decided to fly, but not together. Sky wanted to go down to Los Angeles to visit his mom. So he and Daisy took that route while I flew with the money back to New York. It was probably stupid of us, but we decided to put the money in a duffel bag with clothes and stuff to look nondescript. That meant I had to check the bag, which of course could then get lost. Somehow we didn't consider that and we didn't have a better idea. So onto the baggage belt it went with over two hundred and fifty thousand dollars in it.

Daisy and Sky carried five to ten thousand dollars each on them and I had about the same in my Moroccan bag that I carried on my shoulder. It was a leather bag, like many of the Moroccan men carry, except that this one had long leather tassels and beads on it and was crafted as more of a hippie bag. As I was about to get on the plane, there was a big commotion and suddenly three or four plain-clothes policemen or FBI agents appeared. They were very anxious about something, and of course I was sure it was me. One of the agents spoke to me abruptly.

What's in your bag?

Before I could answer he grabbed it, searched it, and found the money. I was certain that I was busted. I hardly got a chance to react before one agent said to another:

"He's got a lot of cash but nothing else."

They looked at each other and scurried off. They moved on quickly with intensity, without noticeably directing any more attention to me. That apparently was not what they were looking for. I boarded the plane shaken to my core. I was well aware of what was checked in the duffel bag and spent the entire flight wondering what was waiting for me when we landed. When I saw the duffel bag coming down the conveyor belt I was at first relieved that it wasn't lost, but immediately paranoid of anyone in the area. I checked the eyes and body language of the people around and finally lifted the duffel bag off the carousel. I carried it outside where my friend Pete Grayson was waiting. I threw it in the back seat and it triggered no response from anyone. I don't know what that scene was all about, but somehow they forgot about me and moved on to whatever fish they were hoping to fry. That was a very heavy experience…I really thought I was done.

Sky and Daisy came about a week later and Daisy was glad to see me, especially after having heard of my brush with the law. Her love and affection were healing to my spirit. I enjoyed the love as always, even though it would ultimately be painful to my heart. When we were in New Canaan, we stayed at my parents' house. Sky and Daisy stayed together in the cottage and Daisy and I had alone time as well. It was actually easier than when we were in Morocco and together all the time on the same bus. Before heading back to Morocco, we drove up to my parents' summer home on Nantucket to spend a few weeks.

Now we were all back together again in one house and trying to be a successful threesome. At some point, Daisy was on the "abandon me" mode again and I just couldn't handle it. Quite mysteriously, Sofia arrived on Nantucket. She came to find **me** as she had finally broken up with her English boyfriend. But somehow the old flame was gone. Sofia seemed unstable. And what did I expect from an eighteen-year-old girl? And I was an emotional basket case and totally involved with Daisy, so her arrival just complicated things. It felt to me like Daisy was almost hoping things would work out with me and Sofia, but at the same time she recognized Sofia was not right for me, and said so. My heartstrings were frazzled. It was only a few days and Sofia was gone.

I was so messed up that I had to retreat to a friend's house on another part of the island and try to find my head. It was an omen of things to come. It's amazing how you can be in such a beautiful place and be so miserable. Things would not get better; they would get worse. The couple I stayed with were very supportive and kind to me, however, and soon I was functioning again at a manageable level. But it was time to head back to Morocco. We had people to pay and we couldn't safely stay in the USA without risking being caught by the war machine.

We stashed the cash in my parents' basement in the same fireproof box and off we went, flying on a discount airline even though we could now afford better. Daisy had twenty thousand dollars in cash strapped to her, ten thousand to fulfill our commitments to the others who helped us, and the rest to have more than enough to live on for the next year.

Living in Morocco was generally inexpensive and even more so living on the beach at Taghazout (which by the way had grown to about three hundred campers from just eight three years earlier). We used a little propane for our stove and candles for light. We shopped for food at the *souk*, an outdoor market open once a week that is the African version of a farmers market. There were literally mounds of oranges, dates, almonds, and vegetables of all kinds. There were pots, rugs, goats, sheep, cheese, and camels that roared like lions. It was a sensory delight from a visual as well as a culinary perspective. If we spent a hundred *dirham* (about twenty dollars) for the week's shopping, it was a lot. After the shopping, it was on to the *hamam* for a steam bath, a shower, and a shampoo with some kind of mud that left your hair feeling like silk. With my thick hair down to my waist, it was a luxury to get it so clean and feeling so good. Three of us could live on a thousand dollars for nine to ten months…easily.

GROUP OF FRIENDS AND THEIR DOGS IN FRONT OF BIG JOHN

Life on the beach was just about perfect. Twenty years later, I was on the phone making a reservation with a lady at a Marriott hotel in Palm Desert, California when without thinking I answered her question with a Moroccan expression, "Kief, Kief," which literally means "same, same" or "it's all the same to me." I think she was asking me about what kind of a view we wanted, garden or mountain. She was struck by the expression and surprised me with her response.

"I haven't heard that expression in twenty years. Where did you learn it?" she inquired.

I told her about Morocco and she surprised me again.

"I used to live in Morocco, too!"

"Where?"

"On a beach in the south of Morocco."

"Where?"

"Taghazout"

"No way, I was there for three years except for the summers," I said in total amazement.

I hadn't spoken to anyone who knew of Taghazout since we left there in 1972.

"I 'liberated' the road sign outside of the small village one day and I still have it in my garage," she said. *"I loved the life there. You'd wake up in the morning and do some yoga and meditation on the sand dunes overlooking the Atlantic, then go down to Mohammed's café for a cup of Moroccan tea and fresh homemade bread and jam. There was swimming in the ocean, sometimes*

with surf, sometimes still and calm. Shepherds passed by with their herds, sometimes looking for pasture and at other times selling cheese or milk or eggs. On the nights when there was no moon, the sky was so filled with stars that it left you speechless. Passing a pipe while playing music together outside somebody's tent or van; drawing water from the well with that old bucket, and washing clothes in the cement trough; even doing laundry at the well was a pleasure and often a social event. Do you remember?" she said with emotion.

"Like it was yesterday," I replied.

Yes, Taghazout was a special place at a unique time in history, and I could have probably stayed there for a long time except for one thing: something was eating me up. My soul. My spirit was in trouble.

I remember waking up in the morning in our bed on Big John and as consciousness dawned on me, darkness started to set in, like fog at the end of certain Nantucket Island days when evening began. It would silently roll in and suddenly you could barely see five feet in front of you. I had always been a rather happy-go-lucky person; not too much bothered me and things seemed to go pretty well. I was never bored and not often unhappy for any length of time. But life had changed. I didn't really know depression as a state of mind so I can't say if that was what I was experiencing, but it seemed darker than that, almost demonic. I wondered if I could ever be happy again. I was living in a paradise and it seemed more like hell. Once the day got going, I managed all right, but the nights were hard and the mornings were worse. I dreaded the darkness coming over me and it came like clockwork every morning as I woke up.

My heartstrings just couldn't take it any longer. One day Daisy loved me, and the next she was distant and responded to my attention with rejection in her effort to divide her affections as evenly as she could. And still none of us were mature enough to talk about it. The Crosby, Stills & Nash song with the lamentation "Why can't we go on as Three" had taken on new and deeper meaning. A desperate thought emerged.

CHAPTER 28

LEAVING DAISY

There must be some way out of here
Said the Joker to the thief
There's too much confusion
I can't get no relief

—Dylan

If I was ever going to recover my life, it became clear to me that two things needed to happen. I must leave Morocco, Sky, and Daisy and pursue some kind of spiritual life connecting me with the Divine. I was certain that I could not recover on my own. I needed help. If there was a God (and at this point I had come to believe there existed some Higher Power) then He could help me and I must make an effort to find Him. Thinking back, I wonder how it is that I came to believe in anything, when at Andover I lost what remnants of belief in God I may have ever had. At college, I was some variety of an atheist, or at most, agnostic, as I assumed everyone else to be. God was not "in the picture," "on the horizon," or remotely existent in any of my thoughts. I didn't hate Him. That would have required His existence to warrant being hated. He just didn't exist, and I didn't care. But unnoticeably, incrementally, from a variety of different experiences over quite a length of time, I found that I had been led into belief.

It wasn't so much that I had been looking for God. It was more like He had been looking for me, for us, like a shepherd goes looking for a lost sheep until he finds it. And it certainly wasn't any religion that I was following. In fact, religion in general turned me off, Christianity especially. Even though Christ was of Middle Eastern descent, I still viewed Christianity as a mainstay of western culture. I saw the USA as the center of hypocrisy, touting moral values while fighting meaningless wars abroad and living prejudicially at home. If that was Christianity, I wanted nothing to do with it or with their God. But He must be somewhere, within me or within someone, somewhere.

Out of desperation, I turned toward spiritual life. I believed at some level that it was my only real hope.

I wanted to leave Taghazout on a good note. I asked Daisy if she would like to take a few days with me alone somewhere before I left. At first, she tried to talk me out of leaving, and cried at the thought. She didn't want me to leave. But she also knew there was something right about it and couldn't deny me the possibility of finding something better. It was a terrible concession to say yes, because while she wanted to say good-bye by taking a nice trip together, she really didn't want to say good-bye at all. But we would go, one last time together.

I packed my stuff, said my good-byes to everyone, and left Taghazout and Big John forever. There was no fanfare, I just left. I think Sky was happy to see me go. I certainly understood that. But somehow we were still friends...amazing.

Daisy and I decided to go farther down the coast about two hours south of Agadir to some lonely beach near nothing. We found such a beach, with not a single house in sight, where we pulled off the road and parked the van. Maybe it should have scared us a little to be so alone, but we were on a type of honeymoon again together. The only downside this time was that it would end our relationship, rather than begin it. But for the next five or six days we forgot about that and just enjoyed being together, which we always did when the opportunity presented itself. Daisy and I were attracted to and interested in many of the same things. We liked eating healthfully and cooking together. We loved the beach, the water, and the surf. She was spiritual in roughly the same way I was. We were both discovering the Divine and finding the value of investigating the deeper meaning of life. We had the same core values. She also loved Amos, who was with us, since I would be flying home right after our trip.

I don't know what we did to fill our days, since there was nothing to do except enjoy each other. And somehow we did that with ease, cooking and eating three meals a day, playing and sunning on the beach, talking, reading, a little yoga, and intimate time together. I wasn't much of a photographer in those days, but Daisy allowed me to snap a bunch of frolicking, nude photos of her on the beach. When later I had a friend develop them, there was nothing on the film. I never figured out what I did wrong, but it was a unique moment and a playful experience for both of us. It was to live in my memory, not on film.

The days flew by and stood still at the same time. And then it was time to go. The tears flowed as expected, but I think we both knew it was for the best. But something unspoken had happened: Daisy had fallen in love with me. I felt it, and we had experienced it together as the days continued, though it was almost unconscious. It gave me a lot of relief for the terrible moment in front of me. I was leaving the only woman I had ever really fallen for, but I was ready, if that were possible. I boarded the plane in the small airport in Agadir, destination Paris then a change of planes to New York. I waved to the love of my life as she stood near the runway and my plane took off. I tried to see her standing there waving and blowing kisses and crying for as long as I could. And then she was gone, and I wept until I was empty. Drained and exhausted emotionally, I slept. Ah the divine relief that sleep brings. The next phase of life was beginning and I was hoping to find peace again. I had a plan.

CHAPTER 29

RETREAT TO MAINE

*The real voyage of discovery consists
not in seeking new lands*

But seeing with new eyes

—Marcel Proust

My friend Angelo from Grenoble had married a girl named Marie. They had a baby boy they called Daiji and were living on the Canadian border in Calais, Maine. More importantly, Angelo's brother was a Buddhist monk, and Angelo and Marie were serious about spiritual life and meditation. I decided it would be a logical place to pursue my spiritual mission. Angelo was attending a boat building school and he was in the process of building a small boat on his own. I joined him in that endeavor and also took cabinet making, welding, and mechanics. It was January in northern Maine so life was largely confined to the indoors, but I heard about a one-armed man who cut trees and ran a sawmill by himself. I love to work outdoors, so I went and helped him. In the process, we cut some ash trees down and that was where we got the stern board for the boat I was helping Angelo to build. Additionally, I got some pine for some cabinets that I needed for my VW bus. I built them with all dovetail joints and no nails. That's how much time I had.

JUSTIN AND AMOS HELPING MARIE LEARN TO SKATE

Most importantly, I was faithful to my pursuit of spirituality. I stopped doing any drugs of any kind: no hash, no weed, no alcohol, no cigarettes, no nothing. Getting stoned didn't fit my current journey, and perhaps that is why it had seemed to lose its effect on me. The long-term effects of cannabis were little known at the time, but today it is believed that one's drive or motivation may be diminished. Maybe I sensed that I needed all the incentive possible to rediscover life. I brought about a pound of hash with me, but just shared it with others who were happy for the gift. I meditated every morning in a room that was upstairs, next to my room and the woodworking room. I would try to blot out all my thoughts and find the light within or without or wherever the Force might be.

After a month or two, my meditation morphed into something like prayer. When the thoughts would quiet, I found myself silently talking to

God about everything that mattered, past and present, then "download-ing and listening."

Equally therapeutic was working in the woodshop, making my cabi-nets. While I sawed and fitted, I listened to a lot of music of many genres, rock, jazz, folk, etc. I brought my albums with me. But surprisingly, what I found myself most captivated by was Handel's *Messiah*. I liked some classical music and was familiar with Handel's music, but I had never re-ally listened or noted the words before, except the "Hallelujah Chorus." I had managed to take note of the one word, "hallelujah." I was sur-prised and fascinated by the extensive presentation of the story of Jesus Christ over the course of that entire musical work.

As a kid I went to church every Sunday for about five years, yet I knew nothing about the history or teachings of Jesus Christ. My parents made me go and I was only interested in socializing with my friends. Now, the music and the words of Handel captured my spirit. I was deeply moved by the different pieces and though I didn't really get the story clear, my prejudice against Christ began to be broken down.

I still didn't like the religion of Christianity, neither the hypocrisy that I witnessed growing up, nor the more recent version of that, the "Jesus Freaks." They would accost you on the street whenever they could to tell you that Christ was the Only Way; if you didn't accept Him, you would roast in hell forever. Who would ever want to have anything to do with a God like that? I was majorly turned off by them, their approach, and their God. That kind of religion would make an atheist out of an honest person.

The other religions of the world didn't help much, either. They all seemed to have their issues. If someone was looking for God and expect-ing perfection from Him, the world religions just didn't make the grade. I am sure I was overly critical at the time, but it seemed to me that they all taught their own religious superiority and looked down on those who didn't agree with their beliefs. There was lack of logic in their worldview and origins. They seemed more focused on the importance of adhering to dogma or disciplines than a relationship with God and love of our fellow man. I recognized some spiritual potential in the eastern gurus, but many of them turned out to be frauds and their lavish appearance and lifestyle seemed to me contrary to God or true spirituality. Maybe I just hadn't found the right guru yet, the true manifestation of God. I was open, but suspicious.

Meanwhile, my heart had begun to warm up to Jesus, the little I knew of him at least, from Handel's *Messiah*. And the beautiful, moving music: it must have been the result of some kind of divine inspiration upon the talented Handel. I listened to the entire piece at least twenty to thirty times. I knew all the words. The Beatles, the Stones, Jimi, Janis, Traffic, Dylan, the Dead, Santana and many, many more got their time, but Handel fed a part of me that was hungry, very hungry.

And then the first letter from Morocco somehow made its way from Taghazout to Calais, Maine. It had a little picture that Daisy drew of a new moon with the evening star above it. I felt her in the little drawing. Inside was the first real love letter I ever received. It wasn't mushy stuff, it was Daisy letting her heart speak clearly for maybe the first time. Something happened in those last days together and she was different. I had become her light, her evening star, her love. And things were now different between her and Sky, though she couldn't pinpoint how. But what she talked about was us and her feelings and that she longed to come see me. I would only receive two or three more letters over the next few months, but she set an approximate time to come. She wasn't leaving Sky, but she was coming alone, whatever that meant. It would be in late-April. An unexpected event was about to surface that would change everything, however.

Boothbay Harbor

Angelo's course at school was coming to an end and he needed to find a job because he was running out of money. He planned a trip down to Boothbay Harbor, Maine (one of the boat building capitals of the world) to look for work. We drove down together in his truck named Hope in early April. Along the way we got stopped by a cop while I was driving. I don't remember why we were pulled over. Maybe the cop saw two bearded hippies is this old, boxy truck, and assumed some violation would emerge.

"License and registration," he uttered sternly.

And before I could get it into his hands, he said rather gruffly, *"What's your name?"*

"Just in Case?"

I answered as a question, making sure he got the irony. He looked at me funny and asked abruptly,

"Where do you live?"

"On Weed Street," I replied.

With that he got angry and ordered me out of the truck. I tried to calm him down by telling him to look at my license and insisting that I wasn't being sassy, though I was. He looked at my license and there it was: Justin Case, 244 Weed Street, New Canaan, Connecticut. I explained to him that my dad named me after my mom's father, and never realized the play on words that my first and last name became. And Weed Street, well that was just the way it was.

"Sorry, officer. That's the name of the street where I live."

He grumbled and muttered a little, walked around the truck and never told us why he stopped us. He silently sent us on our way. We laughed all the way to Boothbay. How did I ever end up Justin Case on Weed Street?

We arrived late at the house of Angelo's friend in Boothbay Harbor. He warned me just before arrival that they were heavy Christians, but they were nice and wouldn't bother us. They were asleep when we arrived. I noticed quite a few Bible verses written on plaques or notes on the walls. There was one that bothered me. The others seemed nice enough, spouting wisdom or love. The one that bothered me I'd heard from the Jesus freaks and it offended me. "I am the way the truth and the life, no man comes to the Father, except by me." With their *One Way* signs, whenever they approached me, their message was, "There is only one way to God and it is through Jesus. You must accept Jesus as your Savior or you will go to hell. He is the *Only Way*." Their pressuring techniques had a reverse effect on me. I felt more against Christ as a result of the encounter. I considered myself open-minded, on an active search for God and/or spiritual things at this stage. But I was definitely not of the "*One Way*" mentality, and the words of Jesus on a little plaque in their house brought up only negative feelings.

I had been observing that beliefs often alienate and create walls. I noticed that some of the angriest, most prejudiced people I met expressed the strongest beliefs. Their intellectual convictions often had little or nothing to do with what was really important to me. I could not see the value of a belief that didn't reach the heart and make someone a better person. If that belief could translate into a change of heart at someone's core, then fantastic. And Christians, Buddhists, Muslims, Hindus and Atheists, etc., if their beliefs made them more gracious, more forgiving, more loving, more sensitive to others, and less self-centered...then that is admirable. But all the Jesus one way stuff, to me it was dogmatic and arrogant, creating prejudice and alienation, more damaging than helpful. I still think it is what rightfully turns many people off to God. Connecting with the Divine is very personal and unique to each individual. I know that many want nothing to do with spirituality that feels forced, and I didn't, either. That kind of God is not worthy of devotion. I went to sleep, ready for an argument.

CHAPTER 30

THOMAS, KATY, AND AN UNUSUAL CHURCH

"Does that mean that all roads will lead to you?"
"Not at all. Most roads don't lead anywhere. What it
does mean is that I will follow any road to find you"

— The Shack

The next morning was Sunday morning. At breakfast I discovered that Thomas had attended Lake Forest College, in the class just below me. He and his wife Katy were actively involved in a church and they were hippies in appearance and background. I immediately challenged them on this one offensive verse and they listened to my complaints. I told them that I had met some of the most godly people I had ever known in Morocco, where everyone was Muslim. "They were more 'Christian' than most of the people who went to church where I grew up. And what about all the people around the world who had never heard of Jesus, or if they had, it was either as a swearword or some fanatic missionary. How does God deal with them? Can't they know God or come to Him? Sorry, I don't buy your exclusive message!"

Thomas and Katy were not argumentative, and appeared to be listening. Besides, they were hippies so I could relate to them more easily. I usually only argued with someone from the Establishment, so this was new territory. But Thomas had a gentleness about him and we sort of hit it off, so they survived my attacks and, frankly, what I considered reasonable logic. We had nothing to do that day and thus succumbed to their invitation to go to their church in nearby Wiscasset. They guaranteed it would be different than any church from my childhood. It was the first time I had been to a Sunday church service since I was a kid. And it *was* different.

I will always remember Sereno. When I walked up the stairs into the lobby of the church, I was warmly greeted by a number of people. It was 1972 in Maine and I was a very long-haired, bearded hippie, dressed as I always dressed and people were being friendly to me. And it seemed genuine. But then there was Sereno, at least six foot, eight inches tall, heavy but not obese, just big. No, huge. And when he saw me his eyes lit up and his voice rang out, "Praise the Lord," like he knew me or something. Then he stuck out his hand to shake mine and I felt my hand, petite inside his mitt of a hand, and he gave me a big bear hug. "Welcome my brother. So glad you came to join us this morning. Welcome, welcome, praise the Lord!" Someone else it might have offended…all that friendliness…but I enjoyed it. It was real. A smile emerged on my face, but I was speechless, a little shocked I think.

The church inside the doors from the lobby was packed, much larger than my home church, and very much alive. As we were led down the aisle to find a seat, people were shaking our hands as we walked past them. I felt like the prodigal son coming home, in the sense that these people seemed to be happy I was there. They found us a couple of seats toward the front on the right and we settled in. The service wasn't too extraordinary, except the pastor preached from the Bible. I had never really heard anything from the Bible except the Christmas and Easter story, so this was new for me. I heard verses from all kinds of different books of scripture, none of which made much sense, but I found it interesting in some way. And then there was an altar call. Once again, this was a first for me. With every head bowed in prayer, the pastor rambled on for a while in what seemed at first like a long prayer, but then morphed into an appeal to come forward and give your life to Christ and accept Him as your only Lord and Savior. This was way too much for me. I had a book full of reasons why I couldn't take that kind of a step and waited for the appeal to end. A dozen or so, young and old, came forward and then the service came to a close shortly thereafter. We were introduced to a few young people about our age and went home for lunch.

I am not sure whether it was my inquisitive/argumentative approach, or that they thought they saw a genuine heart response in me, or something else, but Thomas and Katy arranged for a regular flow of different people to come by and visit over the next three days. While Angelo was out hunting jobs, I was being wined and dined in a religious sort of way. I remember four people in particular. Yes, Sereno came by. He was a warm and friendly boat builder, with a personality as big as his body and a vibrant faith in God. Then there was a hippie guy and girl, not related to each other, both about my age. The guy was a bit aggressive and engaged me in spiritual debate; the girl was just the opposite. She did not think that an argument was going to convince me of anything and kept defending my point of view, urging the other guy to listen to what I was saying. It wasn't so much that she agreed with my Buddhist-eastern point of view, but she felt that listening was a better approach than debate; she had a broader view of things than the average Christian. Although I did not care much for her friend, she impressed me. *Her* Christianity I could embrace.

Next was the Maine mechanic. If you know anything about the culture of Maine at that time, it was considered to be a backward part of the country, the exact opposite of California. Everything was about ten to twenty years behind in Maine, at least that was the general perception of the rest of us from the east coast. This eighteen-year-old kid was a conundrum to me. He shared with me a bit of his life story, nothing exciting, except for the light in his eyes when he talked about Christ. What was confusing for me was that I had traveled the world and he'd never been outside his own county. I had smoked pot, dropped acid, and had my mind psychedelically expanded. He'd had a bottle of beer. I had graced the halls of higher education. He'd been to high school in Maine. I considered myself spiritually advanced with experiences that he could never have dreamed of, and yet he seemed to have something that I didn't have. How could that be? He was an eighteen-year-old Maine mechanic! Was this young man some kind of social phenomenon or was his spiritual experience real? I went to sleep that night pondering this mystery.

When I awoke, I wanted to get back home to Calais. I wanted to make sure I was there whenever Daisy made the next contact, possibly even this week. But there was a definite stirring taking place inside me that was undeniable. I didn't say anything to anyone, but I was troubled. Troubled because I had questions that didn't have satisfactory answers, but also because I felt something genuine was going on. I wondered whether the Divine that had been in my life at some level was making Himself known to me.

Thomas suggested that I talk to the pastor. I agreed, but I wanted to start home Wednesday, April 12. The only time available was at or after a 6:30 a.m. prayer meeting on Wednesday morning. Now I hadn't seen 6:30 in the morning since my gambling days at Lake Forest when we played all night as a regular occurrence. But to get up at 6:30 in the morning to go t0 a prayer meeting so I could talk to a pastor? Well, if you knew me then, you knew that something was going on for that to happen!

Wednesday morning came after a surprising night of restful sleep. I had more questions than answers, but I sensed that Someone was watching over me, and unlike the last two nights, I fell asleep at peace. Angelo, who was an early riser, came along with Thomas and me for some unknown reason. Maybe he had his own curiosity, maybe he was wondering what was going on with me, but I was glad he was there. Thanks Angelo for being a good friend.

There were about twelve to fifteen people there and the pastor started going on about Jesus's love and how He was the only one who truly loves everyone. It being an informal setting, I piped up and said,

"Well I love everyone." After all, we were the love generation.

To which he retorted with a mild rebuke.

"You don't love everyone. Your love is selective."

Surprisingly, a little voice inside me concurred, reminding me that I didn't love cops, I didn't love establishment people, or prejudiced people, or closed minded people, or people with lace-up shoes or…OK, I got the point. The meeting went on for about twenty minutes with me making a few comments and the pastor keying in on my thoughts. We ended with prayer. It was, after all, supposed to be a "prayer meeting." But the pastor directed the prayer after a few moments toward me and once again brought it around to inviting me to accept Christ as the "only Son of God." Once again, I was stalled at the "only" qualification and the pastor took another tack. He had been talking about the two trees in the garden of Eden and the symbolism of both during the meeting. Now he said directly to me while we were all bowed in prayer,

"Justin, wouldn't you like to stop feeding at the Tree of knowledge of good and evil and start feeding at the Tree of Life and accept Christ?"

I didn't know exactly what that meant, of course, but it sounded good; it felt like something I wanted. The spiritual movements of the last few days, maybe the last few years, pushed themselves to the forefront and I said yes.

"Yes I want that."

"Then accept Christ as the Son of God."

In wisdom, the pastor avoided the "only" hurdle and I took the leap. At that point, I broke down and cried. Like any good cry, there was a lot involved; too much to explain, but part of it was definitely relief. I felt like I had been standing for a long time on one side of a wall and I had finally stepped through to the other side. But since I had never been on the other side of the wall, everything was still uncertain and foreign. I knew nothing about this side of the wall. I was alone. But I had stepped through the wall with some kind of very small faith.

I must have cried for quite a while, for when I was finished the only one still there was Angelo. They had all gone off to breakfast at some café and I told Angelo I would meet them there in a few minutes. I walked down to the side of the Wiscasset River, stood there listening to the river for a moment, and then prayed my first prayer to Christ. It was rather unusual, but very honest:

"Lord, I'm not sure whether you are God or the devil. I believe I have done the right thing. But if I am going to serve you with all my heart, then You are going to have to deal with my many, many doubts."

I found my way to the café as I still had an appointment to talk with the pastor. After a glass of OJ, I said good-bye to Angelo, who would continue looking for a job. Thomas took me back over to church. I joined the pastor alone in his office. I really only had one burning question:

"If Jesus really is the only Son of God, God who became a man, then how does he deal fairly with all the people in the world who don't know Him, never heard of Him or perhaps have encountered Him in a negative light?"

I recounted to him our experience in Morocco and how I found it impossible to connect a loving, just God with the idea of Christ as the only way to eternal life.

"God will judge fairly," he said.

His response was not really satisfactory to me, but not disastrous, either. I left with that mediocre explanation.

I was ready to hit the road. Thomas gave Amos and I a short ride to what he considered a good spot to begin hitchhiking back to Calais. He got out of his car and by the side of the highway he stood with his arm around me and prayed. It was short and to the point. He asked God to watch over me, to make Himself known to me, and to give me good rides home. What was in store for me in the next few days would more than answer that simple prayer.

CHAPTER 31

AUNT SUSIE

Most people want to be circled by safety, not by the unexpected. The unexpected can take you out. But the unexpected can also take you over and change your life. Put a heart in your body where a stone used to be.

—Ron Hall

I wasn't expecting a lot, but the first day it took just two rides right to the town where I wanted to spend the first night. My friend, James Robinson, had moved from New Canaan with his new wife and child to this small town in Maine. After being dropped off, I went to the post office, one of two buildings that made up the center of town. No one knew where James lived as he had a post office box but no street address. I randomly chose one direction out of town, started walking in that direction and waited for a car to come by.

Given that the downtown of this metropolis had two buildings, it took a couple of minutes for a car to appear. When it did, it was a big early-sixties Chevy that looked messy inside and out, as did the mother driving it and the kids in the back seat. She drove by with a glance and disappeared down the road. A minute or two later, she was coming back down the road, and then another minute or two and she was back again. This third time she stopped. Now I could see clearly clothes, bottles, and food strewn around the back seat with three toddlers among them (no seat belts in those days). She was alone in the front seat. She looked at me through the passenger side open window. There was a silent pause that asked *what do you want?* So I asked:

"Do you know James Robinson?"

With a strong Maine accent she replied, *"Nope, I don't know him."* I thought she was going to drive away, but she spoke up again.

"But I heard talk about a family from down east that moved into a house out of town somewhere in this direction."

She volunteered to give me a ride, and five or six minutes later she dropped me right at the driveway of James's house, in the middle of nowhere. I was quite impressed. God had done a pretty good job: two rides right to the small town and within minutes, the most unlikely ride, right to the front door. It was a good first day of the rest of my new life.

I had a nice evening with James and his wife, drank some of his homemade beer, and shared stories including my opportune rides to his front door. They weren't into spiritual things at the time, and of course Christianity for most of us hippies was at the bottom of the list. So I didn't say anything about what had just happened to me. Additionally, even though I wasn't drinking or smoking, I thought it would be a little weird, or at least unappreciative, to refuse the offer of his homemade brew. It was maybe the best beer I had ever had and the last full glass of beer I would have for decades to come. A good way to finish my beer drinking years.

The next morning, after a satisfying homemade country breakfast, Amos and I were off again. James gave me a ride to the main highway and I expected a repeat of the previous day. That would get me home by midday. My quest to know the Divine had been going on for some time, and I had been very earnest for the last six months. Having just made this giant leap to follow Christ…well…I expected Him to show up for me. My faith was weak, my prayer down by the river was real, and my need and my desire to know that I was on the right path was genuine.

There is a verse in the Bible that I didn't know at the time in which Jesus says that if you have a desire to do what is right, you can test Him and find out whether He can be trusted. John 7:17. In other words, God declares that if our hearts are open, He welcomes us to investigate; in that process, we will discover the truth about what He is like, and how real He is. Another verse says, "Taste and see that the Lord is good." Ps 34:8 And another, "Come and let us reason together." Isa 1:18. Faith is not something blind, it is the result of testing, of tasting and experiencing God's reality and His goodness. I didn't know the scriptural background to all this, but I believed it in my heart and mind. If there was a God, then the process of discovering and building faith must be connected to life's experiences, common sense, and logical reasoning. God had come through for the first leg of my little journey, so now I *was* expecting a lot. I got just the opposite.

All day long I experienced short little rides and long waits in between until it was almost 4:00 p.m. and I was still more than sixty miles away. To avoid a long cold night outside, which I was totally unprepared for, I would need a good ride. Then a rather nice man stopped and I was hopeful, but he said he was only going a little way up the road. We drove a few miles until he stopped for gas and I said I would get out there. I got the idea in my head that if someone came in for gas and I approached them personally for a ride I would have a better chance. But he told me that he knew a very good spot to hitchhike from. He said it was sheltered, a nice convenience since it was beginning to snow. I tried to tell him that I preferred to stay at the gas station, but he was insistent. He had been so nice and was so persistent, it felt as if I had no choice. I succumbed to his will.

We drove a few miles outside of town where he dropped me off and headed down the road. There was a deserted ice cream shop, like a Carvel, except older and rather run down. It was set back from the road about a hundred feet and offered a bit of shelter. By the time cars reached this spot, they were cruising at top speed and had less interest in stopping. I would have to run back and forth from my covered spot to the road every time I would see a car coming. It seemed to me it was a terrible place to hitchhike from. There were only two houses that were even visible, one way off in the distance behind me and a little shack across the highway. Nobody likes to pick up a stranger on a lonely stretch of road! I was upset at the guy for offering his ridiculous advice and angry with myself for taking it. Now I was stuck in a poor location, with less than an hour of sunlight left.

It was not easy at that time for a bearded, long-hair to get a ride in Maine, so I had all my hair stuck up under my knit wool cap. At times, Amos could be a help hitchhiking because he is cute, but now with it snowing he was more of a deterrent. Who wants a wet-footed dog in their nice car? So I started pacing as the clock ticked away and I began a conversation with God. I don't remember if I was speaking out loud. It felt like it, because I had a lot of complaining to unleash:

"So here I am Lord, out on the highway in Maine, with my dog, with the sun going down and I don't see any real future here if I don't get a ride soon. I've had lousy rides all day long and now I am in this worthless spot because some guy insisted it's a great place. And I'm running back and forth to stay under cover, which isn't really cover and Amos is following me and getting wet."

Meanwhile, the few passing cars continued to whiz by, leaving a lonely silence behind them as they sped away into the distance. Suddenly, the silence was broken from the shack across the street. A little old lady poked her head out of the front door and called out in a high-pitched, little old lady voice:

"If you want to hitchhike from over here, you can come on over." Quite automatically, I yelled across the highway:

"No thank you, but thank you very much. I don't want to risk my dog running back and forth across the road."

Her shack was on the wrong side of the road for the direction I was going.

I continued complaining to God, running back and forth when the occasional car came by and watching the relentless arrival of dusk. Again the high-pitched voice caught me by surprise from across the road.

"If you want a sandwich, you can come on over."

Once again, like most men on auto pilot who need no help, I yelled back,

"No thanks, thank you very much, I'm OK."

Another few minutes went by with me pacing along the highway; I was tired of running back and forth. My complaining was reaching a pinnacle.

"Did you bring me out here to freeze and be abandoned on the second day of my life with You? Is this what I am to expect of You?"

Suddenly I was stopped dead in my tracks. Like I said, I don't even know whether I was speaking out loud and I don't know if what I heard was out loud, probably not, but it might as well have been. The words were very clear.

"Look, if you are going to complain and ask for my help and I put an answer right in front of you, then you need to take advantage of it. If she has offered you a sandwich with the sun going down, then she must be prepared to put you up for the night."

The logic was compelling. Maybe my ranting had made me blind to the offer and the potential. It was the first time I heard the voice of the Divine in such a clear way (or should I say the *thoughts* of the Divine).

There was no argument. Amos and I crossed the road together and knocked on her door. She was there quickly and invited me in to the little foyer. Then, to my surprise, she took the hat off my head before I could stop her. All my hair came pouring out and I thought she might be frightened.

"I'm sorry, don't be afraid. I've got long hair, but I am not dangerous."

To which she immediately replied,

"Oh that's OK, I have a friend who has long hair, too."

At that point she disappeared into the next room. Before I could get my coat off, she was back with a picture of her friend with the long hair. It was Jesus.

"Look, He's got long hair, too!"

The next five minutes might have been half an hour. I barely breathed there was so much intense, excited exchange between the two of us. This was the first genuine Christian I had ever come across on my own.

"Do you know what just happened to me, not even two days ago?" I blurted out.

Susie was eighty-seven years old, living alone in this little shack for a long, long time. Her Bible was open on the table facing the road. She had been sitting there, her eyesight not good enough to read anymore, but she could see me across the road.

"A still, small voice inside me said, 'Why don't you try to help that young man?'"

Of course she was afraid, all alone and feeble, and me a bearded stranger.

"And then a new thought came to me," she recounted in her sweet little grandma voice. *"How many more times in my life would I have the opportunity to help someone?"*

So she gathered the courage to call out to me. And then of course, at my first rejection, she would have to regroup and determine whether she'd done enough or should "go the extra mile." And the thought came to her to offer me something to eat. When once again I rejected her offer, she just sat back down at her table and prayed.

"If it be Your will, Lord, send that young man to me."

And Susie began to recite by heart what was on the page of her open Bible on her table, now in front of me.

"Let not your heart be troubled: ye believe in God, believe also in me. In my Father's house are many mansions: if it were not so, I would have told you. I go to prepare a place for you. And if I go and prepare a place for you, I will come again, and receive you unto myself; that where I am, there ye may be also."

Susie went on for quite a few more verses until she paused, trying to remember. I continued on for her, reading from her Bible for another minute or so. Then I stopped, stood up, turned around, and hugged her. We both stood there in an affectionate embrace, feeling the warmth of her wood-burning cook stove, and even more than that, the tenderness of the moment. It seemed the most divine moment that I had ever experienced. Neither of us cried; there was too much joy and awe. She made me that sandwich, we shared our life stories, and she became my aunt Susie forever. Hers was a story of hard work, helping her husband log with a team of horses. He died seventeen years ago and she continued logging as long as she could, into her seventies. Then she was strong. Now she was shriveled up and petite, but her heart and her spirit had not diminished.

As expected, she put me and Amos up in the extra room, and I lay in bed that night in wonder of all the pieces that had to fit together just right for me to end up at Aunt Susie's. It struck me that while I was outside complaining to God, Susie was at the same time having her own conversation and inspiration. It was a lesson I have had to learn over and over again: that often when things look dark and almost hopeless, there is a solution brewing, the Divine is already at work. And I couldn't stop marveling at the senseless insistence of that man to drop me off at that forlorn spot. Some people believe angels will occasionally take on human form for a specific task. It's possible in my mind. This much I know, without that man, I would never have had that experience with Aunt Susie. And what if she hadn't pushed past her warranted fears and found the courage to step out of her comfort zone, twice. How a little act of bravery can change the path of life sometimes!

The next morning Susie was up early. If you remember, I mentioned there were just two houses that were visible from where I was hitchhiking. Susie announced confidently that she had a hunch. She called the guy in that other house and sure enough he worked and commuted to Calais every day; he gave me a ride to my front door. At this point, I was surprised at nothing. We said our good-byes with a clear sense of the Divine upon us and I promised Aunt Susie I would come by if I was ever anywhere nearby again. In fact, I would see her one more time.

CHAPTER 32

RETURN TO CALAIS

"Toto, I have a feeling we're not in Kansas anymore."

—L. Frank Baum, The Wizard of Oz

A s I shared the hour long ride with Herb to Calais, he must have thought I was high on something. I don't think he'd ever met a hippie before, and surely not one that went on and on excitedly about the events of the last few days in relation to a spiritual quest woven into the events of the last few years. I was thankful Aunt Susie had been taught by the Spirit not to judge by my hippie appearance. Very few people can see below the surface and not allow cultivated fears and prejudice to dictate. She took a risk and got the reward of a very special moment and an unusual experience in the mysterious workings of the Divine. Who would have thought what was happening in my soul below the surface? It made me wonder if it all could have happened any other way.

Herb, on the other hand, was glad to get me out of his car, especially when we arrived in Calais. Calais was an ordinary looking town in Maine—nondescript, not ugly, but not striking to say the least. It was a gray morning and no sign of spring yet. Everything seemed to have a new brightness to it, even Calais of all places. As we pulled into town I said to Herb with some considerable excitement:

"Doesn't this place look different? I mean it looks totally different to me, vibrant, or more alive or something. Don't you think so, Herb?"

Herb glanced over at me. He didn't answer. I'm sure it looked like the same old dreary Calais to him, on another workaday morning. I'm also quite sure he was relieved to let me off at my front door. I thanked him sincerely for the ride and I thanked God for the door to door service with Aunt Susie on the way.

Marie was home with their one-year-old son, Daiji, which means "great compassion." Her excitement at seeing me was nothing compared to my enthusiasm about my discovery. She was on her own spiritual journey and more than casually interested in what I had found. We talked for some time and I could tell something was happening in her own heart. Angelo came home in a few days, but life did not return to normal. My experience was real and they could see it and we shared much together. My excitement for God was infectious and Angelo and Marie were open. We encouraged each other in our search for the Divine.

A knock came on the door a day or two after Angelo got back. It was a fellow from the boat building school who was maybe ten years older than us and very straight. His name was Bob Johnson. He had short hair, a button-down, collared shirt and lace-up shoes. I don't believe he had ever been outside of Maine. He had come to our door once before, a month or two earlier, and I don't remember why, but he didn't come in. He just stood outside the door and talked with us. Probably we didn't invite him in, but I remembered the conversation. He talked about spiritual things, but he wasn't selling books and he wasn't a Mormon or a Jehovah's Witness. He knew both Angelo and I espoused some sort of walk with God, but was curious as to its nature. We shared a few views about God and spirituality and then he asked us a strange question.

"Do you guys keep the Sabbath?"

I didn't know what that meant exactly, but I knew it was some kind of spiritual exercise so I answered, "Yes."

"What day do you keep it?" he continued, a bit surprised at my answer.

"We keep it every day," I responded, not to be outdone and recalling that every day was "church," in a way, on Big John and that if it was something good to be doing, why not do it daily?

With that, the conversation ended rather abruptly and Bob left, a bit befuddled. We all thought he was a bit suspicious, with his shirt and shoes and unusual questions.

That was a month or two ago, and here he was again. This time there was a new spirit in my heart; I felt concerned for him. In my hippie bias, I thought to myself that anyone with short hair, a button-down shirt and lace-up shoes surely needs help. So I asked if he would like to take a walk with me. I thought that I might share with him my recent experience and perhaps I could encourage him in some way. I figured he really needed something. He was so straight!

We walked around town for at least forty minutes to an hour, and Bob listened intently while I shared my journey. After I finally stopped for a moment, Bob said that he was a Christian and he had a set of Bible studies that I could have that I might find interesting. He brought them by later and I gladly accepted his gift. The irony struck me; he ended up helping me when I had judged him unfairly.

There were twenty-eight studies, and I devoured them. Three days later, I saw Bob and had a question for him.

"Hey Bob, do you have any more studies?"

He thought I had just done the first study and explained to me that I should continue with the second.

"No, I've finished all twenty-eight, do you have any more?"

A bit shocked he promised me a book about Jesus's life, but no more studies. He brought the book by later and once again I thanked him for the gift. I didn't get into the book at the time, however. Daisy was coming.

CHAPTER 33

DAISY ARRIVES FROM MOROCCO

I soon realized that no journey carries one far unless, as it extends into the world around us, it goes an equal distance into the world within.

—Lillian Smith

Marie got the phone call. Daisy was on a plane from New York to Bangor, arriving "tomorrow." The moment had finally come and I was excited to tell her about my new spiritual journey. That said, I was conflicted about a conversation I'd had with Bob who gave me some biblical principle about not having sex outside of marriage. I trusted Bob as genuine, and I was familiar with society's standard, of course. But we, the flower children, were the free love generation, and had completely discarded such a Puritan idea during the sexual revolution of the 1960s. In any case, I was conflicted.

The next day I drove to Bangor to meet the plane. Daisy was wearing a flowing, multicolored, semi-sheer dress that I had bought her, and she looked ravishing. She probably could have been wearing a sack and looked ravishing, but the dress added to her beauty. It felt so good to hold and hug her. As we rode back to Calais, Daisy was cuddled up next to me on the bench seat of my VW bus. It didn't take long before I began the history of my spiritual journey of the last few months, and especially the events in Wiscasset and Aunt Susie. I knew the subject of Jesus would be met with some prejudice and resistance, as we were all rightly suspicious of Christianity based on our backgrounds growing up, and more recent experience with "Jesus freaks." But she knew my previous prejudice, and I told her that the real Jesus was nothing like what we imagined. She listened with an open mind and heart, and she trusted me. I was as intentionally gentle, as I understood well the prejudices that confronted her. She could easily see I was different; a journey had ended and had begun at the same time. What it all meant, neither of us knew. I only hoped she would find the same faith. And I knew that was not up to me.

The two-hour drive passed in a moment and we were back at Angelo and Marie's place. We spent a nice evening with them, cooking and talking together in the kitchen. Then it was off to bed. The sexual conflict resurfaced, which made our first night together not what I imagined it should have been. I was unsettled to an extreme, so much so that the next night I set the conflict aside and made a nice fire in the wood stove in my room. It was a very special time together. Subsequently we sort of decided not to have sex again until we figured things out, and we didn't figure things out for a long time.

We began to study the Bible together and Daisy's prejudice began to diminish. She realized that Jesus was more Arab than American, which made it easier to visualize his character, having lived in and loved Morocco for the last three years. And what was so amazing about Jesus was that he completely crashed the idea of a God so holy that we bow down to him in mindless devotion and surrender of all that we have to Him. Instead, He came to serve and love and to share His life with us. Even more than that, He became one of us, poor and hard-working. He inspires us to love and to live life abundantly, to balance self-love with love of others. His power and majesty are awesome, beyond our scientific and intellectual understanding. But His character of love, the core of who He is, is the most stunning revelation for a human to discover.

Could there really be such a reality...a loving Creator who longs to be involved in our lives? The possibility was growing in our minds and hearts.

One day, while we were studying and processing what we were reading, Daisy rather abruptly stood up. Unbeknownst to me, conviction was growing in her soul, but she struggled with the Christianity she had known and observed. It seemed to her narrow minded, intolerant and judgmental. She turned and started down the stairs. I said something insignificant to her from the top of the stairs and suddenly she stopped, midway down the stairs and began to cry.

"I can't believe that God turns out to be so humble, one of us in a way. It's how I always thought He should be and yet I never thought to consider Christ."

Her prejudice melted before the humility of such a God who lived among us as a commoner and treated all classes with honor and respect. Christianity was not supposed to make us feel superior, it was to make us feel equal, without barriers of race and social status, like our generation had tried to promote. Though someone might be advantaged or disadvantaged in some way, that did not affect their value or equality.

She would fight Him no more. Her desire to know the purpose of life was stronger than her prejudice. She embraced who He was with joy. We were united in faith. We were on this new journey together.

CHAPTER 34

PROVIDENTIAL TRIP TO CANADA

Coincidence is God's way of remaining anonymous.

—Albert Einstein

The next day we planned a trip to Cape Breton, Nova Scotia to look for land. Canada was perhaps going to be our home if the war continued and there was no amnesty. We had heard that Cape Breton was beautiful and more temperate than some parts of Canada due to its proximity to the gulf stream, even though it was pretty far north. It had flowing, rolling hills, woodland of mostly pines and fir, and a spectacular coastline. We headed to an area about an hour south of Sydney called Baddeck, slightly inland from the coast. We just drove around for a while until we came across a beautiful meadow with a river running through it. We were captured by it, so we stopped and knocked on the door of the nearest house. It turned out to be the owner himself. He invited us in and we got acquainted. He was about seventy and lived with his daughter, who was in her midthirties. We shared our desire to build a home in the area and do some farming. We explained our situation with the war and the draft. They were simple and kind folk, with no thought of selling their land, about two hundred and fifty acres of mostly woods. Thirty acres, however, was beautiful meadowland with a large stream running through it.

We offered them fifty dollars an acre and they said they would think about it.

We drove around the rest of the day and found nothing that we liked more. We spent the night in the VW bus and went back the next morning. Apparently, they liked us and could use a little money. We bought it on the spot, right there in their house. They had a deed that they signed over to us and we had twelve thousand five hundred dollars in cash. We could all envision being neighbors, and there was a warmth to our new friendship. It was about three o'clock on a Friday afternoon when we pulled out of their driveway.

As we got out to the highway to head south back to Calais, a thought came to our minds. We had learned from the Bible that the Sabbath was intended to be a day of rest. It was a part of the Ten Commandments and thus must have had some significance that we hadn't quite figured out yet. In any case, rather than driving home that day, we wondered if there was a church nearby that met on Saturday. We did what we did in those days, found a phone booth and the yellow pages in the phone book. Sure enough there was one church that indicated it met on Saturday, a Seventh-day Adventist church in Sydney, just an hour north. So we turned the VW bus around and headed north. That turn, that moment, had much more significance than we could have imagined. I often wonder about how much of my life has been led. I often wonder how the Divine is involved in the seemingly small decisions of life that turn out to be monumental. I wonder if it has anything to do with learning how to listen.

Sydney was a small port city where you could catch a boat if you wanted to go to Newfoundland, which we didn't. We parked on the street right outside the church and spent the night. The church was small, but fitting for the community. We showed up for the service, which was led by a pastor who was from India with a pleasant warmth about him. He spoke that day about the importance of health and quoted an author (E.G. White) who was an apparent expert in the field. Daisy and I smiled at each other knowingly, almost a little excited. Here's why:

In a tent on the beach at Taghazout, sometime in the last four months, a girl showed Daisy a vegetarian cookbook that she raved about. On the cover was a nice looking lady, but with a rather sterile appearance, as she was sitting in a white dress like a nurse or something, reading a Bible. What does the Bible have to do with vegetarian cooking? But Daisy was very impressed with the contents. The cookbook was called *Ten Talents*, and Daisy mailed off an order from the beach in Taghazout to some small town in Minnesota and gave them my address in Calais, Maine. The book showed up requiring a COD payment of $12.50! Now there were VERY few vegetarian cookbooks at that time, but the price tag of more than twelve dollars was extravagant to my mind. The two or three cookbooks we did have were like three dollars each. What was so special about this cookbook?

The knowing smiles we gave each other that morning at church were because we remembered arguing very briefly about whether to pay for the cookbook and Daisy prevailed, citing its extraordinary contents. We perused it outside the post office in Calais and noted its extensive recipes of all kinds and quite a lot of health information included. It was written by a Dr. Hurd and his nurse wife, probably the lady on the front. But it also quoted a number of times from this same author (E.G. White) and there we were in Sydney, the last stop before Newfoundland, hearing about health in a church with quotes from the same author. The coincidence was noteworthy, but nothing compared to what would take place in just a few moments.

As we were exiting the church, the pastor engaged us with some friendly, introductory-type talk. He noticed a tract in Daisy's hand that she had plucked out of the literature rack in the foyer. There was a picture of a fairly handsome businessman on the front.

"That man is from the States, too," he said with a little enthusiasm, as if we might thereby know him.

Since I was in church, I kept my sarcasm in check, but I wanted to say, "There are only two hundred and fifty million of us and I am supposed to know this guy?" But more politely I said, *"Oh really, where in the States is he from?"*

"Connecticut."

Well that narrowed it down to three million people!

"Oh, we are from Connecticut, do you know what town?"

"Yes," the pastor replied, *"New Canaan."*

"That's our hometown!" Daisy and I said at the same time. *"How do you know him?"*

"He and his wife and family come here every July. They own a summer home in Baddeck."

The stunned look on our faces brought a momentary silence to the encounter. Then we told him, almost quietly, that we just bought a two hundred and fifty acre piece of property in Baddeck, yesterday! At this moment we felt there was a plan unfolding before us. This was getting personal! And who was this mystery man? "Yves Federspiel," he said. Although we knew many people in New Canaan, we had never heard that name before. The name was unusual enough for us to remember it at a later date. We should have known; Yves Federspiel would play a major role in our future life.

The pastor and his wife generously invited us home for lunch. I wasn't a great fan of Indian food, generally too spicy for me, but it was all vegetarian and home-cooked which was a treat for both of us, the cherry on top of an auspicious trip to Nova Scotia.

We returned to Calais and the next big event was the arrival of Sky and Daniel, the same Daniel who was with us in Morocco and helped us pack the hash. They were returning from Morocco and due to arrive sometime late in the week. As it was, they arrived Friday night and having just passed through customs, they were clean of any drugs; they knew that I would have an ample stash of hash. What they didn't know was that I had developed some unusual convictions. I had stopped doing any drugs for months, but had no qualms about them getting stoned. However, it was Sabbath! In my new faith, I had a rather narrow, orthodox view of the Sabbath and what one was permitted to do or not do on that day. They had the misfortune of arriving Friday night after sundown, which marks the beginning of the Sabbath.

"So what?" queried Sky and Daniel.

I briefly explained to them my new conviction.

"What has that got to do with us?" they retorted.

It was a reasonable question, but somehow I felt that if they were in my home and since I had the hash under lock and key, they were just going to have to abide by my rules.

"It's not really your house though, it's Angelos!"

"Yeah, but it's my hash," I said.

"No, it's OUR hash," said Sky.

And he was right on that point, but I stuck to my conviction; right or wrong, they weren't going to get the hash till after Sabbath. Sky and Daniel watched the sun go down the next day with keen interest. Immediately the hash was released and they lit up pipes in celebration.

CHAPTER 35

NEW CANAAN, FEDERSPIEL, AND THE DRAFT

*Every story has an end, but in life
every end is a new beginning.*

—*Uptown Girls*

My younger sister and I had always been close. We especially bonded on a cross-country trip in the summer of 1963. I had just turned sixteen and received my driver's license the day before we left; I was looking forward to taking my turn at the wheel. Unfortunately, I was banned from driving on the first day because my older sister Susan and my mother thought I didn't allow enough time for me to return to my lane after passing a car.

My mother and Susan usually sat in the front seat, with Kaylee and I in the back. The car was without air-conditioning and driving across the Midwest was brutally hot. The air coming into the windows only served to keep the hot air flowing, but had little to no cooling effect. Finally, we complained enough to convince my mother to investigate getting air-conditioning installed. It was four hundred and fifty dollars for a normal air-conditioning system, or thirty nine dollars for a system that plugged into the lighter and blew cool air out from ice you placed inside it. We were an economical family, so thirty nine dollars it was. We rolled up all the windows and soon it began to be hotter in the back seat than before. Up front, Susan and mom were getting a little relief from the minimum cool air blowing from our new plug-in air conditioner. As the temperature in the back seat increased, we cracked the windows for a little air. Immediately from the front seat came corrective action.

"Roll those windows up, this AC won't work with any windows down."

We didn't argue with the authorities up front, but Kaylee and I began to strip in our first effort to survive the heat. Then it was face down on the floor to see if we could pick up any cooler air. Meanwhile, the first class passengers in the front seat were enjoying the ride. Surviving on the floor of the back seat, half-naked, was one of many experiences that bonded us as brother and sister. I always got blamed for complaining too much on that trip. It took us twenty-three arduous days (one way) to make the trip up and down and across the USA, visiting all the places others desired. The one and only sight I wanted to see, the Grand Canyon, was scratched from the agenda. We had run out of time.

Back to Maine, 1972. Daisy and I heard that Kaylee was coming to visit my parents at home in New Canaan. I knew she was a seeker and currently into the Maharishi Mahesh Yogi (The Beatles' guru). I wanted to tell her about my recent experiences. We packed up, said good-bye to Angelo and Marie, and the four of us headed home to New Canaan. First stop: Aunt Susie. It was great to see her and rehash the Providence of that evening. Everybody loved her. She was spectacular. The next stop was back to Boothbay Harbor and Thomas and Katy's house. It turned out to be Saturday night when we arrived, and thus we all went to church with them Sunday morning. During the sermon Daniel whispered to me:

"This is babbling."

"Just listen," I said.

When it came to that part of the service where the pastor invited people to come forward to accept Christ, the most amazing thing happened. Daniel went forward. When later that day I asked him incredulously,

"What happened?" he told me of an unusual incident he had in Calais. The experience connected to two lifesaving occurrences he'd had in Morocco, apart from the ones he'd shared with us.

"I was alone in the house while you all were away for the weekend. I picked up your Bible in the living room out of curiosity, thinking to myself, 'Wouldn't it be ironic if the only place I am too prejudiced to look for truth is the one place I might find it?'

"Opening to one of the gospels, I began to feel convicted that while I might be right about so-called 'Christianity,' I may have misjudged the man Jesus Christ. I looked up and said out loud, 'OK, God, if you are real and you are there, and you have anything to do with me, surely you can give me one concrete sign of your existence.' Immediately I was taken back to each of those lifesaving instances in Morocco. I saw that it was God who rescued me and I saw each time how He did it. He then put the thought in my head: 'You can walk away and forget all this happened or you can accept my existence.'

"I was stunned and felt like a total fool. I said, 'OK, God, what if I don't walk away? What do you want me to do…cut my hair…go to church?' I don't believe I heard an audible voice, but I might as well have. The impression was that clear.

"Just read My Book."

"I said, 'OK, I can do that.' The more I read, the more convinced I became that Jesus was exactly who He said He was.

"Even though the church and the pastor did not impress me, I had already determined that after my life of publicly denying God, I needed to confess my faith in Him publicly. The invitation at that church was my first opportunity to do so."

Arriving in New Canaan, I was eager to share with Kaylee. She was open and receptive. She and her boyfriend made a decision to begin an adventure with God; later, they were married and worked for a few years for a church in Oregon, where they revealed a charisma, especially among the youth. When Kaylee left and returned to Colorado, I was sort of left without a purpose at home. Then a letter arrived that changed my life forever.

The return address said *Selective Service*. It was from my draft board. It could only be bad news. It had such an ominous feeling to it. I took it to my bathroom upstairs, closed the door, and sat down on the pot to open it. I guess I felt in my own space there. I wondered what I would do. I had new convictions now, not supposed to lie or cheat, and maybe not even supposed to run. I hadn't thought about that moral dilemma yet. I opened the letter. I was stunned by the short notice inside. They had changed my classification. They had declared me mentally insane and given me a "4-F" status, the most coveted status any of us in my position ever hoped for.

I kept looking for more information. How had this happened? I hadn't gone for a psychiatric evaluation, or even a physical, which is the only way you could get a "4-F" classification. Some had gone to extremes to fail the physical. Others had taken LSD to try to fail the psychiatric exam, but in all cases you had to be evaluated to fail. I kept staring at the card that said "4-F." It didn't really matter how it happened, I had been declared "4-F." There were no circumstances in which a person with a "4-F" status could go to war or enter the military in any capacity. They didn't want me and now wouldn't take me even if I wanted to go. And the more I thought about it, the more I felt it was an appropriate classification. I was definitely mentally unfit for war. That phase of my life had just ended in one moment because of one letter; or should I say because of one number and one letter: "4-F." What could all this mean?

I kept a low profile about my new status; I feared that if I got too excited, the word might get back to my draft board and they might investigate a possible mistake. We lived in a small town and the gossip/rumor channels then could sometimes be faster than the Internet is now. Sky and Daisy and I were all living at my parents' house with three dogs and a parrot. Don't ask me how any of us managed. What we did manage was to investigate churches in the area. I think we visited well over a dozen with a few key questions for the pastor or leader. At the top of our list was the same one about how God relates to people of different faiths, or perhaps no faith at all, who have had little or no exposure to (or perhaps negative experiences with) Christianity. We never got a satisfactory answer until one unusual night.

We were sitting around the dinner table at my house—Sky, Daisy, Daniel, and I, and a couple of other friends—when Daisy or I said,

"Why don't we call up that guy we heard about in that church in Sydney. Nova Scotia?"

It took us a few minutes with the phone book to remember his name, but there it was, Yves Federspiel, over on High Ridge Road. We knew right where he lived. It was a wealthy part of affluent New Canaan. We had been so unsatisfied with the answers we sought from the various churches, but we were reminded of the encounter in the foyer of the little Sydney church. Maybe that guy has something for us.

We called him up and a man with some kind of European accent answered. We told him of the rather unusual way we discovered him, and within fifteen minutes he was at my parents' house in his big gray, nice old Cadillac. It was just after dark when he arrived. My parents were away and the room was smoke-filled from pot and hash that our friends were smoking. It was a little dark. Plus, we were all dressed in our djellabas, so the scene was a little ominous for a wealthy, establishment businessman, to say the least. But Yves seemed completely unfazed by it all. Though later he would tell us he was a little shaken by the scene, he was another one of those rare people that had the divine ability to see below the surface. He walked in like he was one of our old friends that had just showed up out of nowhere.

A handsome man, well over six feet, well built, still in his suit, but without his tie, he greeted us with exuberance, which was infectious. His vibrant personality lit up the room and what turned out to be a Swiss accent set him apart from the average New Canaan, Madison Avenue businessman we were accustomed to. After a little while, our friends continued their conversation while Daisy and I pulled Yves into the kitchen to ask him our key question. I was used to calling older adults *Mr. or Mrs.*, but for some reason his warmth and friendliness caused me to call him by his first name.

"Yves, we lived in Morocco off and on for three years. We have met people around the world of different faiths and beliefs. It seems totally contrary to the character of a just and loving God that the majority of people would be excluded from God's grace because of their circumstances, culture, or religion. What do you think?"

It wasn't like we had been on a month-long trip across the Alps to escape from Nazi Germany; but it *had* been a spiritual journey stretching over years. Now, all of a sudden, someone was taking us through the Bible, with text after text, clearly answering our question. God was indeed fair, more than fair in that he had a clear path to Him whether Christian or Muslim, Buddhist or even atheist; all had access. One's circumstances and prejudices would be taken into consideration. My old pet peeve that Christians often misrepresent God turned out to be true. Too often they paint Him as exclusive regarding who He loves and redeems. There was an abundance of scriptural evidence corroborating that God is capable of reaching people of all religions (or no religion) with His Spirit. Just as there are those who name the name of Christ and are far from Him, there are those that don't know His name at all and are very much His sons and daughters. Many people of different religions and philosophies give evidence in their lives that they are imbibing the Spirit of God, though not necessarily in name, due to culture, exposure, or reasons of understandable prejudice. The Divine judge, "does not see as man sees;

for man looks on the **outward appearance**, but the Lord looks on the heart." It was all right there in the Bible.

I felt like I was in one of those divine moments again—at the end, the beginning and the middle of a journey, all at the same time. My commitment to the Divine took an enormous leap based on a much clearer picture of how God loves all people and wants to connect with them. And it would only get better, though there would be plenty of bumps along the way. It's kind of like a good marriage. If you can make it over the rough spots, it will end up stronger, deeper, and more intimate. But it will test you at times.

We had to vacate my house, as it was too much for my parents with the whole group of us. We certainly understood their point. Yves found us a job at a youth camp up in the Berkshire Mountains in New York State where we could pitch our Moroccan tent and work for our meals while we figured out our next step. We were quite the celebrities there, as most of the kids were in their early and late teens wanting to break out and go in the direction we had just come from. They were all clean cut while we were still in hippie attire, but inside we were the opposite. Talk about not being able to judge by the outward appearance!

A black couple came to sing at the camp. He had been one of the musical directors of *Hair*, the famous rock musical of the sixties. She had been gifted with a soulful voice. Some called her "little Aretha." But now they were singing simple Christian songs. It seemed they were overly compensating for whatever they were trying to get away from, but who was I to judge? They were both big personalities and very talented, and running a vegetarian restaurant on the lower east side of Manhattan. Len and Georgia had an amazing story, and we connected right away, so much so that a couple of months later, we started a vegetarian restaurant in our home town of New Canaan and named it after theirs: The Beautiful Way.

Meanwhile, Daisy took my VW van and headed north to Canada with her two most valuable possessions, her dog and her parrot. She had heard about an orphanage there and wanted to help out. It was her

JUSTIN AND DAISY

means of getting away to try to clear her head. She still had two men seeking her affections and she needed space. But on her way there, she picked up a young male hitchhiker. She didn't want to pull over and sleep when she got tired with him still in the van. Instead, he fell asleep, and unfortunately, so did she...while driving. The next thing she knew she was swerving to avoid an oncoming truck and hit the guard rail. The van began tumbling, flipping down the road, end over end and for some reason all that came out of Daisy's mouth again and again was "Praise the Lord." And when the van came to a stop, completely totaled, no one was hurt. When the police arrived shortly thereafter, Daisy was still spouting "praise the Lord," and the police thought she was high on drugs. But it was soon discerned that she was high on the extraordinary escape of everyone, including her dog and parrot. That attempt to start a new life was apparently not in the Plan and back to New Canaan she came, shaken, but alive.

CHAPTER 36

THE BEAUTIFUL WAY

So don't let nobody stop us, free spirits have to soar
With you I share the gift, the gift that we now know
Love is my religion, love is my religion.

—Ziggy Marley

We found a large old house near downtown New Canaan that had been renovated as a community coffee shop by a nonprofit outfit called "Genesis." The project had failed and the house was now vacant. We approached them with an offer: free rent, free utilities, and we would run a vegetarian restaurant during the week and open it as a "coffee shop" on Saturday nights for young people from town to gather and socialize in a wholesome venue. They accepted, and for the next year we ran "The Beautiful Way." It wasn't very successful during the week, but the Saturday nights of music and food were quite popular. I was the smoothie master, blending up many exotic concoctions with creative names (still making them, going on fifty years now). I also held a Bible study one night a week, which ended up with about twenty young people attending regularly. I sort of regurgitated what we were learning in our own studies with Yves every week, and the result, for some, was the beginning of spiritual life.

But the challenges of our three-sided relationship lingered on. We were all living separately, but we saw each other every day and there was no solution in sight. Daisy remained unable to disappoint either of us, and every affection shown in either direction only created new pain. In time she knew it had to stop, but what would she do or where would she go?

We spent that year studying the Bible with Yves, and later, with a Hungarian pastor friend of his by the name of Karoly Szabo. Pastor Szabo was a master teacher and we felt privileged to discover the Bible at such a deep and intimate level. The Bible had always appeared to me like an irrelevant story, sort of like a boring version of Tolkien's trilogy, *The Lord of the Rings*.

I think it may be very difficult for many of us in our busy worlds to find value in the Bible without a good teacher, an open heart, and the right timing in one's life. We had all three, and the results were dramatic. Spectacular, really. From the boring, old, irrelevant book emerged wisdom, truth, and love combined with the first worldview that ever made sense, not to mention prophetic timing to seal one's confidence. After more than forty years, I am still amazed that such a book exists, one that resonates so much with my being and relates so closely to the challenges of daily life. It inspires and reproves, it comforts and it pricks, it teaches and it stimulates creativity. It doesn't give answers to life's issues, but it does give insight and wisdom so you can use your God given innate ability more effectively to make good choices. If I hadn't had the experience of studying it at a fairly deep level, I wouldn't believe what I am writing. It was one of those "you've got to see it to believe it" experiences.

But many people have it, and we all had it together We were all in awe of this book written over a period of almost two thousand years by so many different authors, and yet maintaining a harmony and consistency as if a single hand was directing them. It was the perfect combination of the human and Divine, written by men, inspired by God. Week by week, Sky, Daniel, Daisy, and I would drive to Long Island to Pastor Szabo's house. His wife was an accomplished Hungarian cook and after every study we looked forward to the culinary delights she prepared for us

There were many "aha" moments. One of the most damaging Christian beliefs that keeps the honest-in-heart questioning the existence of a loving God is the idea of an endless place of torture and suffering called hell. This concept could easily make God's Presence undesirable. Much of the Christian world believes in an everlasting hell, and I wondered if it sometimes gives us permission to be vindictive, punishing others who don't agree with what we deem religiously important. Just from a logic point of view, how can a God for whom love is His core characteristic, be comfortable torturing people forever and ever in some horrific place prepared for ongoing terror? And from a justice point of view, how can the evils of one lifetime be worthy of an eternity of excruciating suffering? And could anyone be happy in eternal life with a former loved one enduring never ending suffering in that place called hell? From every angle, the concept makes no sense.

The history of such a teaching has its roots in power and fear, fear in order to motivate people to obey God and His church. But God has no part in that kind of fear. In fact, "perfect love casts out fear." The truth of the matter is we learned that the common belief of an everlasting hell can be biblically refuted. There are many scriptures that state clearly that death is the end result of hatred and abusive, destructive behavior, not eternal life in some place of ongoing suffering. This is one belief that shouldn't even qualify as a belief, and it completely misrepresents the just and compassionate character of the Divine.

Another eye-opener was to discover that rules were not the core message of the Bible. It is the story of God, the love relationship between the Father, Son, and Spirit that we have been invited into, to enjoy and to some degree to mirror in our relationships on earth. The life of Jesus gives us the clearest glimpse into what that love looks like and how it plays out in the human realm. His story is about God reaching out to us in love, about His relationship with us as a caring, loyal friend, a faithful spouse, and a loving, supportive parent: a far cry from a manual of rules to follow, or else.

The result of this whole experience was just the opposite of what I had been led to believe growing up. The "educated" of the world, in prep school and college, only confirmed me in atheism. It fit my social structure, and based on my information and exposure at the time, it made sense. But it's amazing how life events, timing, and an open heart can allow you to see, and how prejudice and ego can make you blind.

One other epiphany could be summed up this way. Religion around the world often creates spiritual pride and significant misunderstanding, giving the Divine a bad rap. In His day, Jesus rebuked the religious leaders with their hypocrisy and control, and in stark contrast, demonstrated mercy and compassion as true godliness. The everyday person who watched Him heal and love caught the reality of this new concept. This was a significant paradigm shift, away from man-made rules and traditions that control and separate to a healing of the heart; away from majoring on the minors toward an empathy for the wayward.

There was a metamorphosis taking place and we were in the thick of it. Fortunately, Pastor Szabo's wife was a great Hungarian cook who made sure we were all well-fed after each study. But a few issues kept confronting us.

CHAPTER 37

THE MONEY, THE HASH, AND NEW LIVES ALONE

It's hard to imagine the freedom we find from the things we leave behind.

—Michael Card

It wasn't as easy as you might think. What should we do with the money? Should we divide it up among the three of us and use it at will? Should we give it away? Invest it? And what should we do with the remaining hash? Give it to our friends, sell it, destroy it? Based on our history, it was understandable that most of our friends thought we had gone off the deep end. We weren't exactly balanced in our new faith as we were just beginning a very different experience and undergoing enormous life changes.

While we were pondering these dilemmas, Roger arrived from the UK for a visit with a new girlfriend at his side, and he was visibly happy and at peace. He didn't have an opinion regarding the money and the hash, but he was curious on how I viewed the Divine and His presence during our adventure. Roger was no novice in life and his question was a poignant one.

"So do you think God as you know Him today was the one involved in helping us in our hash smuggling escapade?"

"Roger, my dear friend, the Divine is not so interested in what we are doing as to how to make contact with us. His Presence in our adventure was an opportunity to not only protect us, but to reveal His Love and to give us time to understand and discover for ourselves who He is."

"Yes, I can believe that, but I don't think you would find the church agreeing with you."

"You probably know better than I that the church, and perhaps organized religion in general, is often out of sync with the deepest intent of the Divine."

"I think most of England would agree with you there," he said with a twinkle in his eye.

"Here's my take. I see the Divine as the great Lover, tracking us, looking for favorable moments to attract and embrace us. But for each of us, there is a different approach. He can't just grab us and say wake up, here I am. I'm God, you better get onboard or else. We might get that message from the pulpit, but I don't see God like that. Besides, our prejudices, our religions, our egos, our fears—we've got all kinds of garbage standing in the way of us recognizing His Loving approach. I'm guessing it is often a very delicate process for the Divine to allure and to ultimately reveal Himself."

"You're sounding a little eloquent. You're not trying to persuade me are you?"

"Hey, Roger, I am just a kid compared to you. What do I know? You have ten times the experience I do. But what I can't deny is that there is a lot more going on than what we see on the surface. Someone has been tracking me for some time now and that same Someone was somehow involved in our lives over the last few years."

"Well I can't disagree with you there, either."

"And though I can't speak for what God does or doesn't do, I'm convinced He's on our side and what we are up to doesn't stop Him from drawing close. I mean, here we are! Five years ago I was a 'couldn't care less atheist' and today I perceive a God of Love at the center of the Universe. I prefer today's awareness, as far out as it may sound."

"So have you got everything figured out now?" he asked, with another twinkle.

"Yeah, right. Our relationship triangle is still a mess. We don't know what to do with the hash or the money. And we have no real plan. Yeah, I've got it all figured out now." I returned the twinkle.

"Any advice?" I added as a genuine question.

Roger was way too savvy to head down that road. I am not sure how he processed my feeble attempt to speak for the Divine, but at least it didn't diminish our friendship. We gave each other a warm hug and it turned out to be the last time I saw him. I wish he were still alive; I miss him. I hope to see him again.

For the three of us, our lives were in a stage of radical change. Our friends were probably bewildered by it all, wondering if there was really anything genuine going on or if it was just another phase. They also knew we were sitting on a pretty good stash of hash and a lot of money. For some reason, they didn't campaign very hard for the money, but they sensed that we might dispose of the hash and tried very hard to dissuade me/us from discarding it. For some reason, I could only find peace by burning it in a little homemade bonfire, and we agreed to that outcome.

And the cash: it was a difficult time with so many changes happening so quickly that I am sure we didn't make all the best decisions. One day, we piled about half the cash into a suitcase and took it to church.

We walked into the office of our little old Hungarian pastor, opened the briefcase, and told him to use it where it was needed most. To say his eyes bugged out would be an understatement. He knew nothing of our past, and we told him nothing except that we didn't feel this money was destined for our personal use.

It was best for us to put it in someone else's hands. The remaining portion we gave away in different directions. It was never about the money and now, with a new direction in life, it just didn't feel like we should build our future with these funds. Our mission had been to do our part to "turn on" the world. It would be misleading to say we didn't care about the money, but it was never our focus. It was just the result of our mission/adventure and we knew it could have turned out very differently. So just as the Divine had been with us, protecting and directing during this past wild journey, now we felt we wanted a clean start. We were putting that part of our past behind us. We would begin a new Spirit-led adventure without the financial advantage from the past.

It turned out to be the right choice. But there was a dark cloud developing. The breakup was looming in front of us.

CHAPTER 38

THE SPLIT

You can't stop the waves from coming,
But you can learn how to surf.

—*John Cabot-Zinn*

Daisy was the first to come to a decision. She would go to a training school in Michigan that taught health and natural healing. Subsequently, I decided to join a married couple, Don and Sonia, and their four children, in Peekskill, NY. They were starting a more grandiose vegetarian restaurant than our New Canaan endeavor as part of an overall ministry. Sky bought a half-length school bus (he called it a "stubby bus"), remodeled it into a camper, and unbeknownst to me headed out to Michigan for one last shot at winning Daisy's heart. He volunteered for a few weeks at the facility where she was attending, helping to run the sawmill, which he would have been quite good at. In the process, he was appealing to Daisy to join him and go to California. Whatever her reasons were, she couldn't take the step, and Sky drove off to California in his camper/school bus. It was late fall of 1973. We had all gone our separate ways, the three of us never to be reunited again.

In Peekskill, I was learning to build houses from Don and doing some tree work, which I had learned from Sky. This helped us pay the bills while we were preparing the restaurant for opening day. I was doing my best to focus on what was in front of me and recover from a wounded heart, with Daisy now out of my life. And I did pretty well. Though I thought of her from time to time, I was involved in our project and I was studying the Bible with my next door neighbor and his wife. They were into eastern religion, as I had been. Jim and Marily would become lifelong friends as I watched their lives transform right in front of me. It helped me through my sadness, as much as it helped them emerge from some considerable confusion with mysticism.

The restaurant and health food store opened. I was in charge of the store and the business savvy that was in my blood began to emerge. Neither the store nor the restaurant were making it financially, as healthful eating had not yet become fashionable, so I started a little natural foods delivery business, which began to take off.

A year passed quickly. I was nearly over Daisy and she must have been over me as I didn't hear from her at all. My eyes were very open to an available female, but none really caught my eye; there weren't a lot of options in the area, or so it seemed. I still had Amos with me. Nothing like a great dog for whatever ails you.

Then, in June of 1974, there was a convention in Massachusetts that we were to attend. I heard that Daisy was going to be there, so I was quite excited to see her when we arrived. She gave me a straight arm as I went to hug her. Apparently, she had been taught to keep her distance from interested young males, and she did a good job of it. Her own father had died abruptly when she was fifteen, and out in Michigan she had adopted to some degree a surrogate father, Mr. Williams. Anyway, I sat down with him to talk a little about Daisy and how she was doing and he basically told me to leave her alone. She didn't need any boyfriend stuff in her head at this time. It was probably good counsel and I accepted it. It helped me to take the next step away from our past and I began to accept the idea that maybe our past wasn't the healthiest anyway. The Divine probably had a better plan.

CHAPTER 39

LOVE AT SECOND SIGHT

*I've got you under my skin. I've got
you deep in the heart of me.
So deep in my heart you're really a part of me.*

—Cole Porter

In August the same year, Don, who had lived in Michigan, was planning to take a van-load of us to a convention at the very place where Daisy was working. As we rode out to Michigan, I talked to him about Daisy. Don had felt I was overly cautious about my interest in Daisy.

"Maybe I am just infatuated with her and it's got nothing to do with love. I probably just need to forget about her."

"I have been infatuated with my wife for twenty years," Don answered, with enthusiasm to counter my musing.

Don always had a refreshing twist on things. Somehow, I honestly arrived without any anticipation of seeing Daisy. It was a rather liberating feeling. It seemed for the first time that I was really over her—until I saw her.

"Then I saw her face. Now I'm a believer. Not a trace, of doubt in my mind. I'm in love. I'm a believer. I couldn't leave her if I tried"

—The Monkees (1966)

"And the way she looked was way beyond compare. How could I dance with another, oooh, when I saw her standing there."

—The Beatles (1963)

"Sugar pie, honey bunch, you know that I love you. I can't help myself, I love you and nobody else." —The Four Tops (1965)

"Those happy hours that we once knew, Tho' long ago, they still make me blue. They say that time heals a broken heart, but time has stood still since we've been apart. I can't stop loving you." —Ray Charles (1962)

"Wise men say only fools rush in, But I can't help falling in love with you. Shall I stay, would it be a sin, If I can't help falling in love with you. Like a river flows, surely to the sea. Darling, so it goes, Some things are meant to be. Take my hand, take my whole life too. For I can't help falling in love with you." —Elvis Presley (1961)

"I give her all my love, that's all I do. And if you saw my love, you'd love her too. And I love her." —The Beatles (1964)

"I want her everywhere and if she's beside me I know I need never care. But to love her is to need her everywhere, knowing that love is to share. Each one believing that love never dies, watching their eyes and hoping I'm always there." —The Beatles (1966);

"But of all these friends and lovers, there is no one compares with you......In my life I love you more." —The Beatles (1965);

I guess you get the point, and then some. I was hopelessly in love and only distraction and separation had kept it in check. But all the reasons I loved her were standing in front of me again, which I won't bore you with, except to say that it is rare to find in one human being such a combination of external and internal beauty and it's hard to say which one is more captivating. Before the weekend was over, I asked her to marry me and she gave me the answer I was expecting. "I'll think about it." Which she did…for five months and still no answer.

I was back in Peekskill, running the store and developing the wholesale natural food distribution business. I got a letter or two explaining her challenges and hesitation. Finally, I wrote her back and let her know that if she was waiting to see if I was her perfect white knight, it wasn't going to happen. I will never be that good. I didn't hear back from her. But Christmas was coming and a small group was coming east for some reason and her mother lived in Connecticut, so she got a ride. Somehow I made it onto the agenda as well.

And so it was, one day in December that Daisy walked into the store in Peekskill where I was stocking the shelves and my eyes lit up at the sight of her. We had a casual embrace, and visited. I discovered that she planned to go home, but come back soon and work in the restaurant for a few days up until Christmas. We talked briefly about some Christmas plans and then she was on her way to her mom's house in Connecticut.

It wasn't long before she was back again, helping out in the kitchen and waiting tables. It warmed my heart just to watch her work and be friendly to the customers. She always was engaging with her natural warmth, and the customers loved her. She had worked in a vegetarian restaurant connected to the mission school in Grand Rapids, Michigan, so she had no learning curve. It was like she had always been there. But unbeknownst to me, something else was going on. Daisy was affected by my dedication and the manner in which I was running the store and wholesale business. She saw a clear focus and direction with my life. Business came naturally to me, and I was full of energy for my area of responsibility. Plus, I enjoyed people and had some knack for attending to or interpreting their needs. Daisy was touched at some level, and her body language showed me that something was going on in her heart.

Christmas Eve in our home town of New Canaan was quite unique. It was a small town of about thirteen thousand and once a year, every year, there was always a gathering on a hill in town called God's Acre, which had three or four churches surrounding it. There was a band that played Christmas carols just as night fell and it seemed like a major portion of the town showed up to sing. That Christmas Eve was one of those magical ones. It was lightly snowing, but not too cold. Old friends were everywhere, but mostly I was in love and Daisy was with me. And perhaps the biggest surprise that evening was some of the carols actually had meaning. I had sung these Christmas carols all through my youth, but never found any significance in them. It was almost shocking.

After the singing, many of us filed into the Congregational church at the top of the hill to listen to the Christmas story and also to hear a professional male vocalist singing a section from Handel's *Messiah.*

How little I had understood about the true character of the Divine. That divinity would come to this earth as a poor, humble carpenter to live life as we know it, when he could have come as a king, reminded me of that conversation with my grandpa. What was really important in life was becoming ever clearer to me: humility more than status, people more than money, relationships more than success. I would be a slow learner.

This was followed by a professional female soprano singing "Oh Holy Night" from the same masterpiece. It all had such deep meaning, having spent that time in Calais soaking up Handel's divine inspiration, and now, understanding a little more of what it meant for God to become a man. None of this was part of my upbringing. I had been to this same church hundreds of times and for me it had little to no importance. Now, in the life and interaction of Jesus with the people of his time, I saw the loving character of the Divine. The mystery and confusion surrounding God and His supposed harsh and exacting character was lifted as we beheld the compassionate, forgiving, and accepting way in which Jesus treated the common people. Instead of being on the side of the pompous religious people who were all about show and status, He was the friend of the outcast, of the rejected of society, the failures, and the humble.

The warmth of the church compared to the cold outside was a fitting symbol of what we both shared. I think we were ready to be married right then and there, though the thought was never mentioned. We were just on the same wavelength and we knew it; it was inspiring. We went to some friend's house after the service for an informal Christmas party and it seemed to them and to us that we were already together. It was one of those magical, romantic, divine evenings that seemed to have a message. But the glaze would come off soon.

Back to work in Peekskill, and all that was really left to do to make a decision was to talk again with Daisy's "father", Mr. Williams. I had already spoken to Daisy's mom, Anne, and been given the green light from her. She was an extremely proper woman, born and bred in England, with manners and the proper way of doing everything down to a science. And even she was putting pressure on Daisy to give me an answer. I can hear her strong British accent, "Daisy dear, you must give that boy an answer. It is RUDE to keep him waiting so long!" Go Anne, right on!

But as I mentioned earlier, Daisy's dad had died at age fifteen and so the proper step seemed to be to talk to Mr. Williams. And I respected him greatly, myself, and desired his support and validation. More than that, we both felt we really couldn't go forward without his approval. Maybe it's because we had been so extreme in our previous lifestyle that now we were perhaps a little too cautious in our new walk with the Divine. But we both felt God used wise counselors as one of his methods of leading, and we didn't trust ourselves based on our rather tumultuous, chaotic, and emotional past. So we went and talked to him together.

He was there in Peekskill, as he had driven the group that had come east together from Michigan. His RV was parked at Don's house at the top of a steep driveway in Putnam Valley, NY. We sat together in the living room, and I can't remember a word he said, except that there were some kind of reasons given why we shouldn't get married. Depression overcame both of us. We walked out of there as if to our own funerals, down the steep driveway, and then down the steep part of Bryant Pond Road. About halfway down we stopped; we hadn't said a word. I looked at Daisy and said,

"I guess this means it's over."

"I guess it means it is," she replied weakly.

And we hugged each other, in tears for some time along the side of the road. We said our tearful good-byes. Whitney Houston was not yet singing, but the words of the moving song she made famous were totally fitting. See if you can hear her:

"If I should stay, I would only be in your way. And so I'll go, but I know I'll think of you every step of the way. And I will always love you. I will always love you, you my darling, you.

CHAPTER 40

DIVINE INTERVENTION AND GRAND CENTRAL

Have I told you lately that I love you
Have I told you there's no one else above you
There's a love that's divine
and it's yours and it's mine
like the sun
And at the end of the day
we should give thanks and pray
to the one, to the one

—sung by Rod Stewart

I honestly can't remember what happened after that, except that Daisy went home to visit her mother one more time to say good-bye before she would take a train and head back to Michigan. And I went back to work in a fog of depression. I didn't talk to anyone about it, including God. It was over and that's all there was to it. I was numb. One of the young leaders from Michigan came by the store the next day and asked me how I was doing. I burst into muffled tears. He asked me what was going on, and I said nothing. I just kept on working. It didn't take a rocket scientist to guess that it had something to do with Daisy as our developing relationship was well known. So he went and talked with Don, who knew nothing of what was transpiring, either, and then they both went to talk with Mr. Williams to see if he knew anything. That apparently took the rest of the day and into the evening.

The next day started with a phone call.

"Where's Daisy?" Don's voice sounded intense and worried.

"Is there anything wrong?"

"Yes and no," said Don, *"but I need to talk to you right away. There's been a serious mistake. Where's Daisy?"*

I told him I didn't know, but I knew she was going to see her mom and then take a train back to Michigan; that was two days ago, so she may have already gone. "Come down to the restaurant right away, I need to talk with you, now." Don was a fun, supportive brother/father type to me, but there was no playfulness in his voice. It was about fifteen minutes from where I lived to the restaurant and I really couldn't come up with a good idea of what was going on. Don got right to the point. He and the other leader from Michigan had talked with Mr. Williams and questioned him regarding his counsel to us. Not only did they disagree with it, but questioned him as to the rationale of his advice. Upon pressing him, they discovered there was a conflict of interest, and were very upset with him and how he had interfered with God's leading in our lives.

I was stunned, but not so much that I forgot to get right to the point.

"Where's Daisy?"

We called her home and found out she took a train into New York City that morning to connect with a train to Grand Rapids. We did some quick investigation and discovered there was a train leaving Peekskill in fifteen minutes to New York. If I caught it, I would just barely arrive in time to intercept Daisy before the next train was due to depart for Grand Rapids...if I could find her.

Needless to say, we made haste to the train station and I was on the train from Peekskill to New York. The train seemed to be traveling at an unusually slow pace. Was the conductor slowing things down for any good reason, or was it just me? We crept the last few miles into the station. My stress level was extreme, but I didn't think about anything except how to go about finding her in Grand Central Station, one of the most famous railroad stations in the world and maybe one of the larger ones. I knew Grand Central well, as I had commuted on the train from New Canaan to New York every morning one summer, with the rest of the fathers commuting each day to the business capital of the world. And I knew it wouldn't be easy. If you've seen *Sleepless in Seattle*, finding someone on the top of the Empire State Building is a piece of cake. Finding someone in Grand Central...not quite a needle in a haystack, but not easy.

I was the first one off the train, which came in at the lower level. I ran upstairs, passing people like someone was chasing me, or vice versa. My plan was to enter the palace-like, five-story hub of the station where the information booth was and the wall with the arrival and departure information to see if there was a train with the final destination of Grand Rapids. But as I went running through the crowds of wall-to-wall people, for some reason my eyes were directed to the broad stairway leading up to the big clock, which looks dominantly over the entire main section of Grand Central. Daisy was standing on the landing below the clock and somehow her eye caught this person running/pushing his way through the crowd, not realizing it was me. And somehow my eye caught her eye as she saw me running and pushing my way through the crowd.

"Daisy!" I called out to her.

It was similar to the scene of the subway station in *Crocodile Dundee* when he said, "I'm coming through" to tell her he loved her (except the crowd didn't allow me to walk on their shoulders). As I made my way to Daisy, I could see her look of surprise, dismay, and joy all at the same time, if it's possible to combine all of those in one look. She knew something earth-shattering had happened, and as I got close, quite a few of the crowd were excited to see our romantic embrace. I'd like to tell you they broke into thunderous applause.

There on the stairs under the famous clock of Grand Central Station, between adrenalized embraces, I told her the story of intervention. As we sat together on the stairs, amidst the bustling activity, we reviewed the events of the last six months, and especially the last few days. The sense of the reality of God honoring our simple conviction to not push our own agenda, but to trust in Him, was richly rewarded. It felt good to see how things had worked themselves out.

We both went to our respective parents' homes that night and crashed hard after an emotionally draining experience. The next day, after the dust settled, Daisy drove her mom's car over to my parents' house and wanted to talk. I led her into the living room and we sat down on a love seat to the left of the fireplace. I guess the passage of six months keeping me waiting, and the events of the last days, had inspired her to do something unusual. Alone in my parents' living room, she knelt down on one knee. "Will you marry me?" She spoke with such an expressive, playful gleam in her eye that I almost laughed. And for forty years I have been able to tell everyone that it was Daisy who proposed to me. I remembered her mother Anne's words and answered with a resounding *yes*. It would have been RUDE to say no. :)

THE DIVINE TRACKER—
WHAT IF

We know what we are, but know not what we may be.

—William Shakespeare

My journey with the Divine has been just that: a journey, one that continues to this day. One that took me from atheism, with no place or need of the Divine, to a recognition that some One was tracking me. And the Tracker was friendly, protective, and involved in the details of my life, at the center of a bigger story. The experience has caused me to wonder if fate, deliverance, intervention, or stunning "coincidences" are God's way of gently making contact, not so loud and obnoxious that it repels or frightens us, but not so hidden that it can be ignored.

The journey has suggested many answers and raised as many questions.

What if our hunger for love and meaningful relationships exists because that is the core of our nature, designed and built into us by the Divine?

What if the Divine is tracking everyone, seeking us with a motive to improve or restore joyful relationships?

What if the Divine Tracker is so respectful of our free will to love or to hate and that He will never violate that freedom? What if that answers in part the existence of suffering and tragedy?

What if God is not about judging our performance but focused on finding a path to our hearts?

What if some churches give such a skewed picture of God that it is difficult for many to believe or trust that God wants to liberate rather than control?

What if differences are invitations to see and respect another perspective?

What if a journey with the Divine resulted in becoming more forgiving rather than requiring a list of beliefs to promote or vehemently defend?

What if a journey with the Divine meant that all of our apparent failures and setbacks became stepping-stones to something better?

What if the love and pleasures we enjoy in this life are tastes of what He intended for us in the beginning? What if sexual pleasure is one of the gifts of the Divine?

What if sometimes our "gut feeling" is the Divine giving us a nudge in the right direction, a built-in compass that we are capable of listening to?

What if Sam's query to Frodo, "I wonder what sort of tale we have fallen into" turns out to be a love story between the Divine and His creation and we are the ones being pursued?

What if everyone has a divine story?

EPILOGUE— WHAT HAPPENED TO US

Only those who will risk going too far can possibly find out how far one can go.

—T. S. Eliot

It is hard to imagine how a couple of hash smuggling hippies could become, at least for a time, conservative Christians. But when the pendulum swings, it rarely stops at dead center. For quite a few years we were very religious in our habits, before the Spirit took us through the process of balancing our understanding of God's character of love with healthy boundaries. And the "religious" phase was not all bad, it was part of our journey. We emerged from it the same way we emerged from our smuggling days: wiser, more compassionate, a clearer recognition of our own frailty, and more determined to have our lives make a difference. That is a story in itself. The Divine led us through many humbling experiences, which realigned us and ultimately gave us a healthy approach to life and spirituality.

Fortunately, the journey for most of us is not short. It gives us time to pass through manifold experiences, disappointments, and failures, and to learn from them. When we were first married in 1975, we lived in a community that taught health principles, ran a vegetarian restaurant, and concurrently reached out to encourage anybody and everybody that came there for help. We made many good friends and met hundreds of interesting people. It was a growing experience with many bright moments, though not without some severe trials. For example, after giving my all for ten years to a nonprofit organization, I was falsely accused and dismissed for theft and was never given the chance to even discuss or investigate the charges. Later, we went through a fire set by an arsonist that burned all the inventory in our business to the ground.

A midlife crisis brought its own multitude of challenges. With a lot of help, my wife and I made it through with a deeper relationship that keeps getting better. We learned that love is perhaps best defined by forgiveness, not just a one time event but an attitude that permeates the core of who we are. Life is a great teacher; there is probably no better substitute. It's not always smooth sailing and sometimes we felt like we were barely holding on. Like Oprah says, we have to turn those experiences into building blocks rather than stumbling blocks. That is what a successful life is made of. Nobody develops compassion and empathy in a vacuum. The process helped us embrace many wonderful principles that became our focus.

For one, we discovered the great value of living in the country and homeschooling our children in a rural, homestead experience. We were very poor, since we had given all our money away and the lifestyle we adopted and the ministry we joined almost endorsed poverty as a virtue. So we heated with wood—cut down trees and split all our own firewood— and with great enthusiasm our children did what they could to help. We drove used cars and repaired everything we owned over and over again. We didn't own much, an old car and a few wedding gifts. We shopped at the Salvation Army and Goodwill and we thanked God for whatever we had. We grew a lot of our own food and canned almost everything. We went to orchards and picked the leftover fruit (still in good condition)—peaches, pears, and apricots. The kids loved it. Our favorite was applesauce, well over one hundred quarts every year.

Most of the time, we were a working, happy family unit. We learned to live on very little, but no one suffered and we are all the better for it today. For all the mistakes we made, our kids knew they were loved and they knew we loved each other. They felt secure in our affection, and it laid a foundation that is a strength in their own families today.

Our children were a huge education for us. When you work so hard at raising a family and still feel like you could have done better, you spend many hours analyzing and reevaluating. I remember one dark time, in the mid-1980s when I was feeling discouraged on many different fronts. I had been an enthusiastic promoter of my faith, my beliefs, and lifestyle. And now I was asking myself the question for the first time, "Do I really want someone to end up like me—is what I have what I would wish on my friends and my children?" The resounding answer was NO. Religion sometimes can make us feel superior and separate us, whereas the Divine sees us all as equal. Life humbled me again, and our spiritual journey changed its focus. New priorities emerged. Joy and a new freedom surfaced. Respecting and appreciating people with their different journeys became a core value. Spiritual arrogance began to disappear.

My focus was divided between the family, building a natural foods wholesale business for a nonprofit organization, and other nonprofit endeavors. It was thrilling to experience the Divine in a very similar way as our smuggling story. Door after door opened with unusual timing. Incredible opportunities emerged. Big mistakes were followed by amazing recoveries. It was very familiar to us, though it seemed to always catch us by surprise and cause us to thank God. As Providence would have it, an opportunity to go into the same business for profit emerged and I reluctantly went in that direction. Reluctantly, because I was devoted to the nonprofit, but as is often the case, it turned out to be one of the greatest blessings of our lives. Even though my new partner took advantage of my trust, the Divine overruled again and turned it into one of my most valuable learning experiences and increased my competitive juices.

In the late-1980s, when my partner and I sold that business, my wife and I had a little money for the first time in fifteen years. We bought ten acres of bare land in rural Connecticut, cut the trees, and built a driveway nearly a quarter of a mile long into the property, using gravel we dug out of a neighboring farmer's field, and spread with a borrowed bulldozer. We built our own house with a lot of help from our friends. We built a barn from the pine trees on our land that we cut on a portable sawmill we rented.

The homeschooling continued, at which Daisy was gifted. We had a horse and the girls became good riders, learning how to take care of animals. We baked our own bread and one daughter had a little bread business delivering her creations on horseback to the neighbors. We never abandoned our interest in living and eating healthfully. In fact, we studied nutrition and physiology extensively and then gave dozens of cooking and nutrition seminars all over the country, hoping to help many to discover a healthier lifestyle. Daisy helped write a vegetarian cookbook. We had a supportive rural church family and we began to mellow. And I must give all of our children significant credit. Learning to see the world through their eyes and listening to their viewpoints pushed us to broaden our horizons and recognize how people can see things so differently and still be on similar paths.

Our lives went through a major change in the 1990s. We started our own import business that developed into a significant enterprise. We have made lifelong friends and have more than just business relationships with many of our customers and suppliers. It took a lot of hard work and focus that took me away from the family a lot. Developing a business and being a good father and spouse was always a challenging balancing act that was not executed as well as I hoped. Some say that I am a good businessman, but I know there were many occasions along the way that without that same guiding, supportive, protective Tracker, our so called "success" story would have been very different.

I am what I am by the grace of God. I am forever grateful for the people, the wisdom, the timing, the "coincidences," the escapes, and on and on that have helped shape and grow our business and our lives. The Divine is much more a part of everyday life than probably most any of us realize, guiding with practical insight if we're listening. And many *are* listening without even being aware of it.

Over the years we have been involved with many nonprofit projects and ministries, here in the USA and internationally. We have the opportunity to go to Honduras with a spectacular group of dentists, doctors, and oral surgeons to bring health and healing to remote parts of the country. I go as a translator, a helper, and to provide some comic relief. My wife goes as a translator, too, but much more. She is good with people, encouraging both the young team members and the ones we serve. We cherish the opportunity as a group to demonstrate to the people of Honduras that despite their poverty and lack of opportunity, they are deserving of our respect for the hospitable people they are, the hardship they endure, and the courage with which many of them face life.

Today, we have three precious children who are not children anymore. Two of them are key contributors to our current business, and one is in the medical field and has her own health care business. We all live in proximity of one another, a great blessing, having been spread out through California, Pennsylvania, and Colorado just ten years ago. And so far, we have six grandchildren. And Don was right, I have been infatuated with Daisy for over forty years now.

As for Daniel, he married, had a family, and worked in spiritual ministry and in business. And Sky, believe it or not, married beautiful Sofia Zaney, moved to Hawaii, likewise had a family, and works in nature conservancy to this day.

And yes, I have had many thoughtful hours rethinking my faith. You have to if you are honest and understand the importance of always remaining open. And of course, life always finds a way to challenge one's faith and convictions. More than a few times I have asked myself the question, where else would I find purpose? Where else does one find the Source and center of Love? Yes, there are many scientific and non-scientific explanations that people grab on to for a variety of intellectual, emotional, and cultural reasons. But I love the question that the movie *The Life of Pi* asks at the end: "Which story do you prefer?"

I prefer the story of the Divine, who is in love and is Love and created us out of love. Yes, it is a fantastic story, admittedly hard to believe from our limited perspective. I have explored it many times and understand its challenges. But so is every other magnificent story. Yet for me, none answer the questions of the Universe so completely, especially when one factors in the existence of love and forgiveness. They are unexplainable mysteries in other prominent worldviews. Then consider the many "coincidences" that often redirect or shape our lives. It seems that if we pay attention, we will recognize the involvement of the Divine in the details of our lives. And it will thrill us. It is a great story. Could it really be true? There is often much more going on than what we see.

For more information or to connect with the author, go to
godhelpedussmugglehash.com